"We are blessed to re
a nation we proudly co
captivating series, accom
guides us through the extraordinary vision, importance dance,
and unwavering fortitude displayed by our founders' fathers
and patriots. Immerse yourself in the inspiring journey within
the pages of *AmeriCANS Who Made America*, gaining deeper
insights into the courageous individuals who willingly risked
their lives to lay the foundation for the land of the free and the
home of the brave!"
—Kerri Brinkoeter, Co-Host of the *LoveTalk Radio Network*

"Beautifully written stories. The book highlights the
accomplishments of all 40 historical figures spectacularly, and
the descriptions never cease to teach you something new."
—Dhruv Amitabh, 13-year-old and
a published author of Short Stories

"This is an amazing book that helps teach us about the
historical heroes who helped shape this country into what it is
today. It gives famous quotes, and an easy to understand broken
down history lesson for each and every person."
—Darsh Amitabh, 11-year-old
published author of short stories

"Richard V. Battle has written an inspirational account of the men and women who went before us to shape America in the 18th century. Their contrasting backgrounds and willingness to serve. Their belief in education, faith, and virtue that gave them the opportunity to make a positive impression on the future of this country. **This is a wonderful, empowering read for all ages. As Battle quoted from Chief Pontiac, "We must never stop until we have fulfilled our destiny."**
—Salina B Baker, author of *"The Line of Splendor, A Novel of Nathanael Greene and the American Revolution"*

"Richard Battle has embarked upon **an excellent historical series of books for young adults designed to illustrate important figures in American history succinctly and to show their respective roles in building our nation.** His first book in the series is *AmeriCANS who Made America: 18th Century — The Birth of the Republic.* He utilizes a broad section of individuals ranging from presidents to signers of the Declaration of Independence, from financiers and the historic people to slaves who also made important contributions to our new republic.

Each sketch is interesting and informative and helps the reader to appreciate better not only what each individual did but also to more clearly comprehend and understand the historical context within which they acted. Taken together, **the information about these remarkable individuals is not only historically valuable to learn (including many little-known facts) but also provides rich, inspirational role models for today's young adults.** By using and taking to heart some of the examples which Battle has provided, young Americans are enabled to visualize better how they could blaze their own paths to success in today's America and to continue the work begun by these AmeriCANS who each faced and overcame challenges to help build a nation where none had existed before.
—Jud Scott, Rear Admiral, USN (ret) and United States Administrative Law Judge, retired

*"**AmeriCANS Who Made America: 18th Century – Birth of The Republic,** presents an introduction to talented and* committed leaders dedicated to establishing and building a new republic free from the rule of the British Empire. You will know some names well and already value their collective efforts.

Others may be familiar, but not their patriotic contributions in war or the creation and building a new republic. Many names will be new and unfamiliar, but they were vitally important to the cause of freedom from the tyranny of a foreign government and the building of a new nation founded on the rule of law rather than of men.

Why are these people and their stories so important to us today? Given the divisions within our historical political parties and the animosity between elected officeholders and challengers in the upcoming national elections, **there is no better time to reflect upon the stories of those leaders responsible for the founding of our republic. Our obligation is to protect and defend the efforts of their work."**

—Gerald Hill, former Texas State legislator

For Victor Edwards
Aim High!
Work Hard!
Never Quit!

Richard Battle

AmeriCANS
WHO
MADE AMERICA!

18TH CENTURY - BIRTH OF THE REPUBLIC

RICHARD V. BATTLE

Headline Books, Inc.
Terra Alta, WV

AmeriCANS Who Made America!
18th Century - Birth of The Republic

by Richard V. Battle

copyright ©2024 Richard V. Battle

To order additional copies of this book or for book publishing information, or to contact the author:

Headline Books, Inc.
P.O. Box 52
Terra Alta, WV 26764
www.HeadlineBooks.com

Tel: 304-789-3001
Email: mybook@headlinebooks.com

ISBN 13: 9781958914373

Library of Congress Control Number: 2024935687

"Now is the time for all good men to come
to the aid of their country."
—*Charles E. Weller*

For all those who risked their "lives, fortunes, and sacred honor" and others, through their life's labors and sacrifices, contributed to giving us the gift of liberty we inherited, may God bless you and rest your souls.

And may He give us the courage to extend this most precious and rare gift to future generations, and may they also forward their legacy.

TABLE OF CONTENTS

Preface... 11
About this Book.. 13
Acknowledgments.. 15
Cover Photo Story.. 16
Our Founding Patriots Blessed Us Greater
  than Our Appreciation of Them 18
AmeriCANS are not a timid people... 22
Republic 23

Founders **25**
  George Washington 27
  Benjamin Franklin... 31
  Patrick Henry 36
  Thomas Paine 39
  Thomas Jefferson... 43
  James Madison 47
  Samuel Adams.. 52
  John Adams 56
  John Hancock
    First signer of The Declaration of Independence.................... 60
  Dr. Joseph Warren 64
  Alexander Hamilton 67
  Roger Sherman... 70
  John Marshall 74
  Samuel Chase 78
  Rev. John Witherspoon 82
  George Mason 85

Robert Morris..88
Charles Carroll of Carrollton 91

Patriots...**94**
John Paul Jones..95
Anna Smith Strong 98
Paul Revere 101
Molly Pitcher 104
Christopher Seider (Snider) 107
Nathan Hale...110
Lt. Col. Benjamin Tallmadge..................................113
Betsy Ross 116
Mary Katherine Goddard 119
Billy Lee...122
Captain John Parker 124
Henry Knox 128
Mercy Otis Warren 131
Francis Marion "The Swamp Fox"..........................134

Leaders..**138**
James Forten...139
Gilbert Stuart..141
Jonathan Edwards 143
Eli Whitney...147
Charles Wilson Peale..150
Daniel Boone...153
Chief Pontiac 156
Phyllis Wheatley..159

A Note from The Author 162
Bibliography..164
Index 166
About the Author 169
Richard V. Battle Books 171

PREFACE

I've loved history as long as I can remember and American and Texas history even more. Over the course of time, people known and unknown to us across history have benefitted us, our world, and the freedom that blesses us in The United States.

While we can't repay those individuals in the past, we can learn from them and return the favor to current and future generations yet unborn.

This work is part of a series dedicated to repaying our forebears in a small way and fulfilling my mission to communicate uplifting messages of hope and encouragement, benefitting people today and influencing future generations. It celebrates *AmeriCANS Who Made America* by recognizing their achievements.

I desire to profile and honor some of those predecessors the reader may or may not know. I hope revealing how everyday AmeriCANS accomplished extraordinary achievements will encourage readers to aspire to more than before they read this volume.

In addition, I believe we can learn invaluable lessons from these individuals and others that will improve our lives by inspiring our imagination and motivating our actions.

Former Supreme Court Justice Oliver Wendell Holmes Jr. said, "A mind once stretched by a new idea never regains to its original dimensions."

It just takes one idea to change a life and influence untold others' lives. We never know when or how that one idea will appear, but if we actively learn from our experience and the experiences of others, we are more likely to multiply our learning, improve the human condition, and exponentially increase our influence on future generations.

WHERE DO YOU GO FROM HERE?
ABOUT THIS BOOK

This volume is one of a series of books celebrating the AmeriCAN-do spirit from the beginning of our great country. While written for young adults, adults will also find valuable insight. I hope *AmeriCANS who Built America* will benefit readers today, add depth of understanding later, and inspire them to expand our prosperity and face any threat to our great country.

This volume celebrates the 18th Century, whose defining moment was the Birth of The Republic. I publish this as the first volume in the series because the 18th Century was, is, and will be the most consequential to preserving and perpetuating our liberty.

Included are profiles of individuals whose actions contributed to building the most prosperous and free country in the history of the world. It certainly is not a complete list, but it is representative of many of our predecessors deserving our thanks.

None of these people were perfect--we are not perfect, nor will our posterity be perfect--but they made mighty contributions to building our great country. Their actions and attitudes reflect the essence of the AmeriCAN-do spirit! We focus on the positive activities of the people profiled despite any setbacks or negativity associated with them.

Because the American Revolution dominated 18th-century America, our Founders and Patriots whose service secured independence from Great Britain are represented in more significant numbers in this volume than others.

The fact is that the actions of a group of unique individuals from all over the colonies worked together to create our blessed country. Believers attribute the success of our Revolution and Independence to God's Providence. Many non-believers credit our founding to random luck or coincidence.

While there are some names we are familiar with in this volume, there are many more, in addition to those whom we include here, whose selflessness and sacrifice deserve our remembrance and honor. They illustrate that everyone who contributed positively to the United States through their labor and family efforts built the country we are blessed to live in. They formed an informal team utilizing their unique talents to achieve a more significant impact than they could have individually.

Our responsibility is to learn from the past, value the uniqueness of America, and strengthen our shared future with our efforts. We mustn't let our failures deter us from maximizing our positive actions to improve the human condition.

Fulfilling our obligations as citizens will pass liberty to the next generation, and our failure will dishonor our forebears and sentence future Americans to lives without freedom.

Stronger AmeriCANS make America stronger. A stronger government makes Americans weaker. The founders confirmed it in the beginning, it is true today, and it will remain valid as long as our nation exists.

Acknowledgments

Anything positive I have achieved is partly due to more people than I can thank here or anyone else. Thank you to all of you who have contributed to my life.

My daughter Elizabeth is the first and primary beneficiary of my efforts to help people win every day, and I appreciate her love and support.

I'm continually grateful to Logan Cummings, my friend, mentor, and former pastor, whose selfless gift of advice, counsel, and encouragement is priceless to any accomplishments I may achieve.

Thank you to Burke Allen, Shaili Priya, and the Allen Media Strategies team, who represent me professionally but have also become great friends and cheerleaders of my mission for their advice and counsel. I also appreciate Dhruv and Darsh Priya for their feedback in the early stages of this project.

I sincerely appreciate Cathy Teets and the team at Headline Books for their faith in me and this project. Their expertise and contributions were invaluable.

Thank you, Alane Pearce, for your invaluable guidance and editing prowess for helping me to communicate my message better.

Cover Photo Story

One of the most famous paintings in American history portrays Washington and the American army crossing the Delaware River on Christmas night in 1776. The successful attack on Trenton the next morning renewed hope in the revolution at a time when almost everyone thought it had vanished.

Emmanuel Leutze's 1851 painting conveyed many emotions that represented Washington and the individual soldiers in the image. Standing in the bow, General Washington displayed the resolve illustrated in the password for the night, "Victory or Death." The audacious nighttime crossing represented a desperate action by patriots compelled to act or abandon their pursuit of liberty.

Washington's perseverance and example, which he demonstrated throughout the war, is evidenced by his facial expression and stance.

The future president and lieutenant James Monroe is the only other passenger portrayed standing, holding the flag for all to see and take hope in their quest.

You can almost feel the weather that night. Dark, cold, and windy, snow and ice clogged the river, forcing soldiers to move it with poles to complete the crossing successfully.

The other soldiers are purposely dressed in a variety of clothes, illustrating the diversity of people who banded together to birth The United States. They discarded their appearance for the little comfort they found in covering themselves with every garment they could secure.

Though not 100% historically accurate, the painting and this cover convey the AmeriCAN-do spirit we inherited from our forebears who built and improved our country generation by generation.

The images on the back cover represent Betsy Ross, Chief Pontiac, The Spirit of 76 painting, and Billy Lee. They are but a few of the individuals and groups described in this volume who deserve our remembrance and honor and who are worthy of our emulation as we live and leave our mark on America for future generations of free people.

The 18th Century birthed our Republic. It continues today, and with God's blessing and every American's contribution, it will continue to shine as a beacon of freedom throughout the world.

Our Founding Patriots Blessed Us Greater than Our Appreciation of Them

Declaration of Independence
John Trumball, 1818
Yale University Art Gallery

In a rush to destroy our history, we often overlook the brilliant men who crafted our **Declaration of Independence in 1776** with logic and reason rather than emotion and anger.

God aligned the stars, and it happened to be 56 white men who represented all Americans.

1. These were serious men who knew what they risked and why, but felt the gamble was worthwhile to create a unique place on Earth where men governed themselves and individual liberty was the order of the day.
2. They risked "their lives, fortunes, and sacred honor."

3. According to *The Lives of the Signers of the Declaration of Independence* by B. J. Lossing, nine died fighting, or from hardship, twelve had their homes pillaged and destroyed by the British, five were captured and tortured before dying, two lost sons, another had two sons captured, and others lost wives and fortunes.

"Give me liberty or give me death."

—Patrick Henry

"We hold these truths to be self-evident, that all men are created equal, that they are endowed by their Creator with certain unalienable Rights, that among these are Life, Liberty and the pursuit of Happiness."

—President Thomas Jefferson

We've given you "a republic if you can keep it."

—Benjamin Franklin

"Liberty, once lost, is lost forever."

—President John Adams

"The greatest tyrannies are always perpetrated in the name of the noblest causes."

—Thomas Paine

"It is in the interest of tyrants to reduce the people to ignorance and vice. For they cannot live in any country where virtue and knowledge prevail.

—Samuel Adams

THESE MEN

1. Were brilliant because they recognized man's imperfections, including their own.
2. Distrusted government realizing its tendency to evolve into a bureaucratic master if citizens surrendered their independence.
3. Sacrificed monumentally to give us individual liberty with political and economic freedom. Those twin freedoms are inextricably intertwined. We either preserve both or lose both; that is our responsibility.

In 1787, the United States Constitution was a brand new document. It is now the longest active governing document globally. The relevancy of their thoughts and writings confirms the immutable **agelessness of human nature** and the brilliance contained in the Constitution and Declaration of Independence. The **Constitution is not a breathing document** that follows changes in human development but is a solid foundation constraining the worst tendencies of humans to enslave people through government.

The writers of the Constitution recognized they didn't give us a perfect government but one they hoped the people would continue to revise in order to "form a more perfect union." Instead, they **correctly understood the inherent nature of humans.**

IT IS OUR TURN

1. We must **execute our responsibility** to sustain our individual liberty and mastery over our public servants.
2. **If we honor our founders** and predecessors, we'll breathe our last breath as a free people, confident we repaid the favor given to us.

3. **If we fail** to stand up to the forces intent on subjugating all people to the rule of man instead of the rule of law, we will enter darkness long before we take our last breath.
4. **Every day** and in every action, we make choices contributing to our future freedom or, eventually, subjection.
5. **It is up to each of us**, therefore, to contribute to the freedom of future generations rather than squander our inheritance.

"If men were angels, no government would be necessary. In framing a government which is to be administered by men over men, the great difficulty lies in this: you must first enable the government to control the governed, and in the next place oblige it to control itself."

—President James Madison

"If ever a time should come, when vain and aspiring men shall possess the highest seats in Government, our country will stand in need of its experienced patriots to prevent its ruin."

—Samuel Adams

"Posterity! You will never know how much it cost the present generation to preserve your freedom! I hope you will make a good use of it."

—John Adams,
Letters of John Adams, Addressed to His Wife

"My only regret is I have but one life to give for my country."
—Nathan Hale

AmeriCANS are not a timid people.

2 Timothy 1:7 – For the Spirit God gave us does not make us timid, but gives us power, love and self-discipline.

Galatians 5:13 - For, brethren, ye have been called unto liberty; only use not liberty for an occasion to the flesh, but by love serve one another. (KJV)

America was born with people imbued with a CAN-do spirit. Their tenacity created a civilization out of the wilderness.

Re-igniting our forebears' spirit will propel future AmeriCAN generations to achieve great things through their God-given Liberty!

Republic

First flight of Old Glory

"Republic. I like the sound of the word. It means people can live free, talk free, go or come, buy or sell, be drunk or sober however they choose.

Some words give you a feeling. Republic is one of those words that makes me tight in the throat, the same tightness a man gets when his baby takes his first step, or his first baby shaves, makes his first sound like a man.

Some words can give you a feeling that makes your heart warm; republic is one of those words."

—Davy Crockett in *The Alamo* movie, 1960

***

"The cause of liberty must be under the protection of Heaven, because the Creator surely wills the happiness of his creatures; and having joined the faculty of reasoning with our natures, he has made us capable of discerning that the true dignity and happiness of human nature are only to be found in a state of freedom."

—Richard Henry Lee

FOUNDERS

John Adams, Thomas Jefferson and Benjamin Franklin read the Declaration
of Independence to, and Benjamin Franklin read the Declaration of
Independence to the citizens of Philadelphia. Filippo Costaggini, artist

"THESE are the times that try men's souls." The summer
soldier and the sunshine patriot will, in this crisis, shrink from
the service of their country; but he that stands it now, deserves
the love and thanks of man and woman.

Tyranny, like hell, is not easily conquered; yet we have
this consolation with us, that the harder the conflict, the more
glorious the triumph.

"What we obtain too cheap, we esteem too lightly: it is dearness only that gives everything its value. Heaven knows how to put a proper price upon its goods, and it would be strange indeed if so celestial an article as FREEDOM should not be highly rated."

—Thomas Paine

"You will never know how much it has cost my generation to preserve your freedom. I hope you will make good use of it."

—John Adams

PRESIDENT GEORGE WASHINGTON

Crossing the Delaware   The Prayer at Valley Forge
Arnold Friberg, 1976

"I cannot tell a lie. I chopped down the cherry tree."

Six-year-old George Washington (February 22, 1732-December 14, 1799) is said to have told his father this famous quote upon discovering the fallen tree. Legend tells us Washington received a hatchet as a present, and wanting to use his new tool, he chopped down the tree.

Human nature is to avoid responsibility and look for excuses or others to blame. Washington's behavior stands out because it is exceptional. Today, the accuracy of this story is questioned by some. Regardless of modern-day doubters, Washington's entire life demonstrated his superior character, making the story's truthfulness believable.

When I was five, I received a toy tool kit with a hammer, screwdriver, pliers, and a real saw. The closest wood in my room was a dresser. Like Washington, I was eager to use my new tool and sawed several notches in the furniture. Unlike Washington, when my dad caught me, I was obviously guilty, and the spanking I received is still memorable. My parents kept the dresser well into my adult years, and it served as an unintended reminder of my misadventure and the whipping.

George Washington is the unrivaled poster child for **AmeriCANism**. He had little ego; he let his actions speak instead of words, and he led by example. Washington saw others' strengths and potential and was skilled in placing people in positions to maximize their contributions.

Washington's survival after having horses shot out from under him and bullets pierce his coat, but not his body, confirmed to him Providence spared him for a greater purpose in life.

Washington›s character was the difference between our nation winning independence and remaining a British colony. When the cause looked lost, his commitment remained steadfast, and he persevered and inspired others to hang tough as well.

As the winter of 1776 approached, everyone believed the Army would rest; Washington knew spring would reveal a failed revolution unless they achieved a triumph soon. So he led the Army across the Delaware River on Christmas night, leading a surprise attack on Trenton the next day. So precarious was the cause, Washington utilized "Victory or Death" as the password. The victory, and one following in Princeton days later, lifted the Army's and citizens' spirits and instilled hope of triumph and liberty.

George Washington was the obvious and only choice to lead the Continental Army because of the experience he gained in the British Army during the French and Indian War. He learned the value of persistence when overlooked for a commission and learned valuable lessons which we benefit from because of the resulting triumph in the quest for independence.

His leadership and integrity made him the only choice as the first president of The United States. He could have been king or president for life—some people were calling for it—but he set aside his ego and voluntarily walked away from power after two terms, establishing a precedent that lasted more than 150 years. He was a servant leader before the term existed. No one deserved the title of Father of Our Country more than Washington. No one was more integral to winning independence and creating the United States than he was.

Praised after his passing, Henry Lee, a fellow leader in the Continental Army, said, "Washington was first in war, first in peace, and first in the hearts of his countrymen."

Citizens so respected Washington that signs saying "Washington slept here" or "Washington dined here" or other variations attracted visitors to those sites for many years.

He was such a great example of a life well-lived; we should remember him always, and not just when we spend a quarter or a dollar and see his picture.

George Washington Quotes

"Happiness depends more upon the internal frame of a person's own mind, than the externals of the world."

"The harder the conflict, the greater the triumph."

"Be courteous to all, but intimate with few, and let those few be well tried before you give them confidence."

"Associate yourself with men of good quality if you esteem your own reputation; for tis better to be alone than in bad company."

"Few men have the virtue to withstand the highest bidder."

"If freedom of speech is taken away, then dumb and silent we may be led, like sheep to the slaughter."

"To be prepared for war is one of the most effective means of preserving peace."

"To contract new debts is not the way to pay old ones.

"A government is like fire, a handy servant, but a dangerous master."

"Of all the dispositions and habits which lead to political prosperity, religion, and morality are indispensable supports."

"It is our duty to make the best of our misfortunes."

"The blessing and protection of Heaven are at all times necessary, but especially so in times of public distress and danger."

Benjamin Franklin

"We must all hang together, or most assuredly, we shall all hang separately."

Benjamin Franklin (January 17, 1706 – April 17, 1790) told this to his fellow signers of The Declaration of Independence using wit and humor to defuse highly stressful situations and make an important point. There was no more serious action than declaring independence from Great Britain.

Franklin and his fellow patriots declared they pledged their "lives, fortunes, and sacred honor" in the Declaration. Failure in the revolution would result in their conviction as traitors and their execution by hanging.

Benjamin Franklin was the oldest signer of the Declaration of Independence and a leader, example, and mentor for the other delegates. His age and lifetime achievements in several fields elevated his influence on Americans, and anger from the British.

***

Franklin's legacy of success makes him worthy of learning his secrets, which will help the quest for our dreams. Born the eighth of 10 children, he knew success depended on his efforts instead of inheritance. Like many other early American exceptional leaders, Franklin only attended school for two years but was an avid reader of the classics providing him with a better education than school could.

He was a proponent of hard work, which became the basis for achieving the American dream. Franklin began as a printing apprentice for his brother, who also published a newspaper. Angry, the paper refused to publish his letter, Franklin adopted the pen name Silence Doogood, whose letters were very popular and further inspired his writing commenting on public events.

Leaving his brother's shop without permission at 17, Franklin moved to Philadelphia, finding varied work opportunities. The Pennsylvania governor encouraged him to move to London with the promise of funding a competing newspaper. Three years later, Franklin returned to America, the promise unfulfilled.

Before Franklin returned to business, he continued his pursuit of knowledge by reading. He created the first public library in Philadelphia to increase access to books because of the expense of acquiring your own collection.

He opened his print shop at age 22 and began writing his almanac in 1733. Readers recognized his critical thinking and writing skills, encouraging his continued growth and opening the doors for other opportunities.

"Never leave that till tomorrow which you can do today," Franklin advised and lived, as proven by his lifetime of many and varying accomplishments. Franklin's professional efforts included:

- **Printer** – He retired from printing (I prefer the term repurposed his life) at 42 years of age. His most outstanding achievements and impact on people's past, present, and future occurred afterward. That example alone inspires us to look every day for opportunities to benefit others positively.
- **Author/Philosopher** – Installments published over twenty-five years, *Poor Richard's Almanack* became a "must-read" for most colonials and should be for every modern American.
- **Inventor/Scientist**-The Franklin stove, bi-focal glasses, the glass harmonica, the Franklin Decision-Making sheet, and other inventions were significant. However, his most famous work was discovering electricity and creating lightning rods to reduce the risk of burning buildings.
- **Statesman** - He served in the Pennsylvania assembly, was the first postmaster general, was the oldest signer of the Declaration of Independence, and was the seasoned leader guiding approval of The U.S. Constitution.
- **Diplomat** - Franklin spent years in England before the war and in France during and after the Revolution negotiating to prevent war, secure the French alliance, and crafting the peace treaty formalizing American independence.

***

Franklin's organizational skills were well known; he kept an appointment book for planning and a diary of his daily activities, increasing his efficiency. His natural curiosity inspired his constant thirst for lifelong learning, producing many benefits that affect us still and will continue beyond our lifetimes.

Among his many honors is he is one of two non-presidents on US currency appearing on the $ 100 bill, and he was also on the less used 50 cent piece.

Words are insufficient in this volume to fully credit Benjamin Franklin's achievements.

BENJAMIN FRANKLIN QUOTES

"God helps those who help themselves."

"Honesty is the best policy."

"By failing to prepare, you are preparing to fail."

"Early to bed and early to rise makes a man healthy, wealthy, and wise."

"An investment in knowledge pays the best interest."

"A penny saved is a penny earned."

"Tell me and I forget. Teach me and I remember. Involve me and I learn."

"Energy and persistence conquer all things."

"Sell not virtue to purchase wealth, nor Liberty to purchase power."

"An ounce of prevention is worth a pound of cure."

"He that is good for making excuses is seldom good for anything else."

"They that can give up essential liberty to purchase a little temporary safety, deserve neither liberty nor safety."

PATRICK HENRY

"GIVE ME LIBERTY, OR GIVE ME DEATH ?"
PATRICK HENRY delivering his great speech on the Rights of the Colonies, before the Virginia Assembly convened at Richmond, March 23d 1775. Concluding with the above sentiment, which became the war cry of the Revolution.

"Give me liberty or give me death!"

If you know anything at all about **Patrick** Henry (May 29, 1736 – June 6, 1799), you will most surely first think of this most familiar declaration. Still, his confidence, commitment, and initiative contributed mightily to American independence in the 18th century and to the freedom we enjoy today.

After trying multiple careers, he studied law and handled many cases showing exceptional talent as a fiery speaker. His speaking skills earned him a seat in the Virginia House of Burgesses at the perfect time, as disagreements with England rose and the need for good leadership arrived.

As a 29-year-old freshman legislator, he ignited the house chamber by speaking against the recently enacted Stamp Act, which increased taxes on the Colonists to pay for British troops in the colonies. Protesting this first direct tax, he said there were no longer distinctions between people from states, and that above all he was an American. His groundbreaking proclamation changed people's perspective of their citizenship, which greatly influenced future events.

In March 1775, Henry attended the Virginia convention called to consider responding to British oppression of the colonies. While some argued patience and inactivity, Henry proposed a resolution for the Virginia militia to defend the colony in case of war. Talk led to more talk, and three days later, the attendees were no closer to a plan of action than when they began the meeting.

As Patrick Henry listened to more idle words, his blood boiled as he prepared to speak. Emotion burst forth as Henry called the representatives to action, stating that inaction was not an option and war had already commenced whether they recognized it or not.

Concluding his argument for proactive movement, he announced with emphasis, *"Is life so dear or peace so sweet, as to be purchased at the price of chains and slavery? Forbid it, Almighty God! I know not what course others take, but as for me, give me liberty or give me death!*

Henry's words left the crowd speechless, but fate made their debate immaterial barely three weeks later; as shots rang out in Lexington and Concord, the time for discussions ended. The hour for the patriots to win independence began.

After a short time leading the Virginia military forces, Henry left to contribute to writing the Virginia Constitution in 1776. He was elected the first governor of Virginia and continued influencing the war effort, the building of The United States, and public debate until 1790.

His thought leadership led some people to call him the Father of the Revolution. Many viewed him as the most renowned orator of the Revolution.

Patrick Henry quotes

"I have but one lamp by which my feet are guided, and that is the lamp of experience. I know no way of judging of the future but by the past."

"The Constitution is not an instrument for the government to restrain the people, it is an instrument for the people to restrain the government – lest it come to dominate our lives and interests."

"The liberties of a people never were, nor ever will be, secure, when the transactions of their rulers may be concealed from them."

"It is when people forget God that tyrants forge their chains."

Thomas Paine

"These are the times that try men's souls,"

Thomas Paine (February 9, 1737 – June 8, 1809) penned these words during the darkest days of the Revolution in 1776 in his work that General Washington used to inspire the troops, *The American Crisis Number One*. Each generation feels it experiences tough times, but none faced the risks of losing "lives, fortune, and sacred honor," as the founders did and stated in The Declaration of Independence.

Unlike most founders, Paine was born in England and didn't arrive in America until 1774. His formal education ended at 13, and repeated failures in his youth and early adulthood gave no one reason to expect anything else from his life.

As in nature, where a tree that survives harsher weather is stronger and produces more and better fruit than one untested, Paine would prove to overachieve expectations. Like other remarkable people, he used his setbacks to build a stronger character, and the resulting fruit is still sweet for us today.

Demonstrating it's never too late to change course and get results in America, Paine helped found and worked editing *The Pennsylvania Magazine*. The opportunity lit a fire in his spirit at the exact time disagreements between the colonies and England escalated.

He wasted little time pushing the colonies to press for independence rather than continued arguments over taxes, representation, and other issues.

After the "shot heard round the world" at Lexington and Concord on April 19, 1775, Paine wrote *Common Sense*, publishing it in January 1776. His case for natural rights, human equality, individual liberty, minimalist government, and a rejection of the monarchy was one of the most persuasive writings that influenced The Declaration of Independence.

Paine served in the Army, and his experience with the shortcomings of the war led him to write *The American Crisis Number One* in December 1776, which included the **"These are the times that try men's souls..."** quote. The paper moved General Washington so much that he read it to the troops and ordered it recited to all American soldiers when many were preparing to leave the Army and go home. Paine's inspiration led many soldiers to stay, enabling Washington to cross the Delaware River and lead the momentum-changing attack on Trenton the day after Christmas.

Continuing his efforts as a thought leader inspiring the patriot's quest for liberty, Paine wrote a total of 16 *Crisis* papers through 1783. He refused payment for any of his wartime writings, demonstrating his servant leadership but leaving him poor.

After the war, he published *The Rights of Man* in 1791 and *The Age of Reason* in 1794 while imprisoned aiding the king of France.

Returning from France in 1802, Paine discovered Americans had forgotten him, and he died underappreciated in 1809. Long after Paine died in 1937, *The Times of London* called him the English Voltaire, leading to a renewed appreciation of his contributions to American independence and individual liberty.

Thomas Paine is a marvelous example that **it isn't where you begin in life but where you finish that matters**. All Americans, past, present, and future, should appreciate his positive impact on our lives.

Thomas Paine Quotes

"These are the times that try men's souls. The summer soldier and the sunshine patriot will, in the crisis, shrink from the service of his country; but he that stands it NOW, deserves the love and thanks of man and woman.

"What we obtain too cheap, we esteem too lightly: it is dearness only that gives everything its value."

"If there must be trouble, let it be in my day, that my child may have peace."

"Character is much easier kept than recovered."

"Arguing with a person who has renounced the use of reason is like administering medicine to the dead."

"Reason obeys itself, and ignorance submits to whatever is dictated to it."

"A body of men holding themselves accountable to nobody ought not to be trusted by anybody."

"The greatest tyrannies are always perpetrated in the name of the noblest causes."

"We have it in our power to begin the world over again. A situation similar to the present hath not happened since the days of Noah until now. A birth of a new world is at hand."

—January, 1776 in Common Sense

PRESIDENT THOMAS JEFFERSON

"Educate and inform the whole mass of the people. They are the only sure reliance for the preservation of our liberty."

Thomas Jefferson (April 13, 1743 – July 4, 1826) certainly practiced what he preached. Despite today's questions about some of Thomas Jefferson's activities, we should not let it diminish the volume and impact of his contributions to establishing our republic and individual liberties.

Jefferson was fortunate to come from a good family. Still, he did not rest on his advantage but continuously worked to improve himself after his formal education and to serve others.

Jefferson continued his lifelong commitment to learning and set a goal of collecting a personal library of 1000 books. He sold 6700 volumes to Congress in 1815 to partially replace books burned in the Capitol in the War of 1812.

His list of accomplishments is long, and his humility appears in his self-written epitaph - *Author of the Declaration of American Independence of the Statute of Virginia for Religious Freedom and Father of the University of Virginia."*

Jefferson was selected to lead the effort in writing the Declaration as a better writer than a speaker. One of the most famous phrases in it states, **"We hold these truths to be self-evident, that all men are created equal, that they are endowed by their Creator with certain unalienable Rights, that among these are Life, Liberty and the pursuit of Happiness."** Jefferson and the founding fathers recognized human nature was unchanging, and people were imperfect. We continue to work *"to form a more perfect union,"* as they stated in the Constitution.

Among his many other accomplishments not on his epitaph, he served in the Virginia legislature, the Continental Congress, as the governor of Virginia, and as minister to the French court.

After the Constitution was enacted, he served two terms as the first Secretary of State under President Washington and as the second Vice President under President Adams. He then served two terms as the third President of the United States. He doubled the size of the U.S. with the Louisiana Purchase and commissioned Lewis and Clark to lead a two-year expedition of the West in search of a waterway to the Pacific Ocean and to learn more about that vast area.

Jefferson believed in limited government and maximum individual liberty based on his extensive studies of previous governments throughout history. He surely could not conceive the size of government we have today nor the sacrifice of liberty citizens have endured as it takes more freedom with each power it claims for itself.

Thomas Jefferson gave us the best prescription for life, saying, **"I predict future happiness for Americans if they can prevent the government from wasting the labors of the people under the pretense of taking care of them."**

Thomas Jefferson graces the two-dollar bill, which many people have never seen, and the five-cent coin, which is used less and less due to inflation and electronic transactions.

ADDITIONAL THOMAS JEFFERSON QUOTES

Government

"Most bad government has grown out of too much government."

"The government that governs best...governs least."

"It is error alone which needs the support of government. Truth can stand by itself."

"Government prohibitions always do more mischief than had been calculated."

Liberty

"If a nation expects to be ignorant and free, in a state of civilization, it expects what never was and never will be."

"I would rather be exposed to the inconveniences attending too much liberty than to those attending too small a degree of it."

"I prefer dangerous freedom over peaceful slavery."

"A republic is the only form of government which is not eternally at open or secret war with the rights of mankind."

Principled Living
"Honesty is the first chapter in the book of wisdom."

"In matters of taste, swim with the current. In matters of principle, stand like a rock."

"It is always better to have no ideas than false ones; to believe nothing, than to believe what is wrong."

"Nothing can stop the man with the right mental attitude from achieving his goal."

"I am a great believer in luck, and I find the harder I work, the more of it I have."

President James Madison

"If men were angels, no government would be necessary. In framing a government which is to be administered by men over men, the great difficulty lies in this: you must first enable the government to control the governed, and in the next place oblige it to control itself."

Though he was not elected president until 1808, James Madison (March 16, 1751 – June 28, 1836) is known as the "Father of the Constitution." His contributions to the founding of the United States cement his standing with our 18th-century heroes.

Madison was born into an established Virginia family, which provided him with a broad classical education. Torn between a career in the clergy and law, he continued his studies and tutored his siblings, both activities that broadened his knowledge and experience. Who knew the depth and breadth of his schooling would enable him to assist the founding and Constitution significantly?

Commissioned in the militia, he left it when he was elected to the Fifth Virginia Convention to create its state constitution. He later served in the state assembly, where he became an ally of Thomas Jefferson.

Adding to his experience, Madison contributed to creating The Articles of Confederation. Later, he realized its shortcomings and pushed for a stronger national government.

Working from his position in Congress, he wrote and spoke, arguing for a new governing document. Madison worked with other Virginia delegates to create and promote The Virginia Plan, which included three branches of government, a bi-cameral legislature, and proportional representation--all essential features of the final Constitution. He collaborated with Alexander Hamilton and John Jay, authoring the *Federalist Papers* and publicly advocating for a more republican government as the Constitution expanded.

His youth, small and unassuming appearance, and non-threatening, soft-spoken manner enabled him to persuade others more easily than his peers in political discussions. Madison represented the old saying, **"It's not the size of the dog in the fight, but the size of the fight in the dog."** In a debate during the Virginia ratifying convention, he surprised many by besting the perceived champion debater, Patrick Henry.

The Constitution embraced Madison's promotion of adding a *Bill of Rights* to it and secured his election to Congress. A long-time proponent of religious freedom, Madison's leadership resulted in the first ten amendments to the Constitution being ratified on December 15, 1791.

It is easy for us to take our individual rights and the restrictions placed on the government for granted. Thankfully, for more than two hundred years, leaders from all political parties and beliefs restrained themselves and each other to preserve our Liberty. Heaven help us when any politician ignores the gift of freedom our founders gifted us in the vain pursuit of unlimited power.

A long-time associate of Thomas Jefferson, they co-founded the Democratic-Republican party, and Madison served the Jefferson administration as Secretary of State from 1801-1809. From his cumulative life and experience and this position, he ran for and won the election as president of the United States in 1808.

The two most recognizable events of his presidency receive mixed reviews. Nearly everyone applauds his leadership in The War of 1812, which affirmed American independence even though it was not a decisive victory. First Lady Dolly Madison is revered for saving the Gilbert Stuart painting of George Washington when British forces burned the White House and other public buildings on August 24, 1814, after overwhelming a small American volunteer force in a skirmish.

Now a player on the world stage, America prospered, unleashing its people's individual ingenuity and ambitions.

Viewed through more than two hundred years of history and cultural progress, many people today view Madison's policies toward Native Americans less positively than Americans saw them at the time of implementation. And, our forebears viewed their results as mixed at best.

Madison left the presidency poorer than when he entered office. He was a faithful public servant, leading the country with impeccable integrity and an example I wish today's politicians would emulate.

He rarely involved himself publicly in politics during retirement but mentored many. He helped his old friend, Thomas Jefferson, establish the early growth of The University of Virginia.

Madison last served in public office in 1829 as a delegate to the Virginia Constitutional Convention to revise the document he had influenced earlier. One of the last surviving founders, James Madison, passed away in 1836 at eighty-five years old.

James Madison Quotes

"The purpose of the Constitution is to restrict the majority's ability to harm a minority."

"The happy Union of these States is a wonder; their Constitution a miracle; their example the hope of Liberty throughout the world."

"Knowledge will forever govern ignorance; and a people who mean to be their own governors must arm themselves with the power which knowledge gives."

"It will be of little avail to the people if the laws are so voluminous that they cannot be read, or so incoherent that they cannot be understood."

"If our nation is ever taken over, it will be taken over from within."

"The truth is that all men having power ought to be mistrusted."

"I believe there are more instances of the abridgement of freedom of the people by gradual and silent encroachments by those in power than by violent and sudden usurpations."

"The essence of government is power; and power, lodged as it must be in human hands, will ever be liable to abuse."

"Oppressors can tyrannize only when they achieve a standing army, an enslaved press, and a disarmed populace."

Samuel Adams

"The liberties of our country, the freedom of our civil constitution, are worth defending against all hazards: And it is our duty to defend them against all attacks."

It is our loss if we only know of Sam Adams because of the beer and not the man behind it. He's been called the architect of the American Revolution. His influence on the liberty and moral character of the United States gifted our ancestors and us with the freedoms we enjoy today.

Samuel Adam's (September 27, 1722 – October 2, 1803) ancestors were pilgrims, and his family taught him about faith, freedom, and natural rights from childhood. Adam's father was a Massachusetts assemblyman and deacon and secured an education in the law for Samuel. His first wife and four children died before the war began.

While he wandered from job to job, his real interests were in politics and the unjust treatment of the colonies. His modest lifestyle and demeanor demonstrated his integrity, increasing his credibility when arguing political points. His training led him to frame debates between good and evil, with liberty and virtue as essential components of good and the tyranny of serving England as evil. He recognized the connection between private virtue and public action in officials.

Earlier than most, he recognized the only satisfactory solution for the colonies was independence from Great Britain. The progression from working, negotiating, and agreeing with colonial leaders to declaring independence lasted more than ten years. Adams and others continually persuaded other leaders of the only natural alternative to peace and happiness. Without their persistence, and later Washington's and others for almost twenty years, we may still be British subjects instead of American citizens.

Samuel Adams was older and more outspoken than most founders, establishing him as a thought leader, example, and mentor. His leadership paved the way to secure our religious and property rights.

Adams influence in creating the Committee of Correspondence brought the colonies together and sped their realization of shared grievances and the benefit of uniting their efforts.

He was a delegate and signer of the Declaration of Independence and continued to serve his country until his age and declining health forced his retirement.

Adams' relentless actions pushing for independence led some to call him the Father of the American Revolution and the architect of liberty and virtue for the United States. His dedication and lifetime efforts are worthy of our honoring his memory every time we celebrate our freedom.

Samuel Adams Quotes

Virtue

"Virtue is the surest means of securing the public liberty."

"Religion and good morals are the only solid foundation of public liberty and happiness."

"The sum of all is, if we would most truly enjoy this gift of Heavean, let us become a virtuous people."

"We may look to armies for Defence, but Virtue is our best Security. It is not possible that any state should long remain free, where Virtue is not supremely honored."

"It is no dishonor to be in a minority in the cause of liberty and virtue."

"Neither the wisest constitution nor the wisest laws will secure the liberty and happiness of a people whose manners are universally corrupt."

"It is sometimes not an easy thing, to persuade a man to believe that to be true, which he wishes may not be true."

"We shall succeed if we are virtuous. I am infinitely more apprehensive of the Contagion of Vice than the power of all other enemies. It is the disgrace of human nature that in most countries the people are so debauched, as to be utterly unable to defend or enjoy liberty."

Liberty and Rights

"Among the natural rights of the colonists are these: First, a right to life, secondly to liberty, and thirdly to property; together with the right to defend them in the best manner they can."

"If we suffer a tamely lawless attack upon our liberty, we encourage it, and involve others in our doom."

"Mankind are governed more by their feelings than by reason."

"But there are some persons who would persuade the people never to make use of their Constitutional rights."

Tyrants

"How strangely will the Tools of a Tyrant pervert the plain meaning of words."

"It is in the interest of tyrants to reduce the people to ignorance and vice. For they cannot live in any country where virtue and knowledge prevail."

"If ever a time should come, when vain and aspiring men shall possess the highest seats in Government, our country will stand in need of its experienced patriots to prevent its ruin."

PRESIDENT JOHN ADAMS

"Liberty, once lost, is lost forever."

John Adams (October 30, 1735 – July 4, 1826) faced the most unenviable task in the young history of The United States. He followed George Washington as president.

Adams and Washington differed in style and personality, adding to his challenge of gaining acceptance and leading the country forward.

John Adams was born into a modest family, contributing to his belief that people should advance in life based on merit rather than the English custom of royal titles and inherited favor.

John disliked studying as a boy, so his father gave him manual labor, showing him his future without an education. Before he completed his first day digging a ditch, he asked his father to return to schoolwork.

He tested and gained admittance to Harvard at fifteen years old and taught school in his first job after graduation before his love of politics and the law inspired him to change course for himself and the country.

He married Abigail in 1762, and she was his closest advisor. Their letters reveal personal and public events of the time, painting a picture for us of the founding and early years of the United States. Though he couldn't speak of it for years, losing a child in 1770 strengthened his character. Their overcoming the devastating loss together set an admirable example for those facing losses in the upcoming Revolutionary War.

Adams loved to learn by reading and observing human nature and promoted others to do likewise. He was a Christian, patriot, and leader in thought and action. He wrote as he talked and enjoyed peace on his farm.

Adams's leadership skills were rewarded with his election to the First Continental Congress in 1774, where his vision and voice trumpeted independence. He championed 17th-century British leader James Harrington's philosophy that "governments should be of laws, not men." This led to his authoring *Thoughts on Government*, which became the guidebook for several state constitutions, including Massachusetts, the oldest written founding document in the world.

By the way, elected leaders in those days often faced election every year. Our founders were wiser than we are in holding politicians accountable to the voters.

Adams's thorough study of human nature convinced him that virtue and the education of citizens were essential for the country to succeed. He strongly believed no effort in favor of virtue was wasted.

John Adams was an early and vocal advocate for separation from England. People called him the *Oracle for Independence.* His ambition for the country and himself led to more than thirty years of service to his country.

He served in the Continental Congress, was one of the last surviving signers of the Declaration of Independence, traveled to France to serve as a diplomat, and was the first vice president and second president of the United States.

John Adams was the first president whose son, John Quincy Adams, later served as president, which was a unique achievement until George W. Bush followed his father, George H. W. Bush, in 2001.

After leaving public life, he renewed his relationship with President Thomas Jefferson, with whom he corresponded actively. Both declaration signers died on its fiftieth anniversary on July 4, 1826.

JOHN ADAMS QUOTES

"You will never know how much it cost my generation to preserve your freedom. I hope you will make good use of it."

"When public virtue is gone, when the national spirit is fled the republic is lost in essence, though it may still exist in form."

"Our Constitution was made only for a moral and religious people. It is wholly inadequate to the government of any other."

"Liberty cannot be preserved…without a general knowledge among the people."

"Those who trade liberty for security have neither."

"There are two ways to conquer and enslave a country. One is by the sword. The other is by debt."

"Power always thinks...that it is doing God's service when it is violating all his laws."

John Hancock

"There, I guess King George will be able to read that without his spectacles!"

John Hancock (January 23, 1737 – October 8, 1793) stated this upon placing his signature first and the largest on the Declaration of Independence.

All the Declaration's signers became traitors to Great Britain when they pledged their "lives, fortunes, and sacred honor" to all Americans in the quest for independence when they added their names to the document.

Hancock's extra-large first signature made a statement and set an example, encouraging the other signers as they bravely committed to giving their all for "liberty or death," as Patrick Henry said. Today, we would say, his remark was an in-your-face comment that boldly spoke to the king. His signature became so well known that others commonly asked us to sign our "John Hancock" on a document.

The son and grandson of ministers, an inheritance from an uncle enabled John Hancock to take time from business efforts and enter politics. His initial service was in the General Provincial Assembly in Boston alongside other future founders.

With the British Parliament's passage of The Stamp Act in 1765, frustrations amongst colonists erupted. Hancock was an influential voice in the Sons of Liberty who mobilized political opposition and civil protests to the law and continued throughout the Revolution.

Over the next ten years, Parliament enacted more laws upsetting the colonists, including the Townshend Act leading to the Boson Massacre in 1770, the Tea Act inspiring the Boston Tea Party in 1773, the Intolerable Acts in 1774 punishing colonists for the tea party, and taking more power from Americans increasingly upset with British actions.

Finally, the king ordered the British Army to arrest John Hancock and Samuel Adams and confiscate weapons at Concord, Massachusetts, on April 19, 1775.

The night before, Paul Revere and others rode from Boston to warn citizens in Lexington and Concord, and Adams and Hancock that "the regulars are out," or as we say today, "The British are coming," calling the American patriots to arms.

The British Army's arrival in Lexington was the fuse that lit and set off the "shot heard round the world" on April 19, 1775.

Hancock and Adams escaped arrest, and the Minutemen's stand and response meant no turning back on the road to revolution and fight for independence.

Hancock fiercely believed in individual liberty, faith, and self-governance by the people. He used an extensive part of his wealth to finance the beginnings of the Revolution, adding credibility to his outspoken voice.

He represented Massachusetts in the Continental Congress from 1775 to 1780 and served for a while as its president. While presiding, Hancock's most famous action was signing the Declaration of Independence occurred.

Hancock later contributed to the Massachusetts constitution and became its first governor in 1780, serving until his death in 1793.

While less known than some founders, his courage, voice, finances, and lifelong commitment to serving his country and citizens contributed mightily to our freedoms.

The next time someone asks you to sign your "John Hancock," know it compliments a great American.

John Hancock Quotes

"The more people who own a little business of their own, the safer our country will be, and the better off its cities and towns; for the people who have a stake in their country and their community are its best citizens."

"Resistance to Tyranny Becomes the Christian and Social Duty of Each Individual."

"I glory in publicly avowing my eternal enmity to tyranny."

"Sensible of the importance of Christian piety and virtue to the order and happiness of a state, I cannot but earnestly commend to you every measure for their support and encouragement."

"A chip on the shoulder is too heavy a piece of baggage to carry through life."

"The greatest ability in business is to get along with others and to influence their actions."

DR. JOSEPH WARREN

"The man who meanly will submit to wear a shackle, condemns the noblest gift of heaven, and impiously affronts the God that made him free."

It is easy to overlook Dr. Joseph Warren's (June 11, 1741 – June 17, 1775) contributions to our liberty because he gave, as President Abraham Lincoln said during the Gettysburg Address, his "last full measure" during the Battle of Bunker Hill (It was actually fought on Breed's Hill next to Bunker Hill) more than a year before the Founders signed the Declaration of Independence.

As a medical doctor, he could have confined his efforts to treating wounded soldiers during the battle. Nevertheless, he fought alongside his fellow patriots as an equal, not a superior, illustrating the difference between British and American culture. Elbridge Gerry, a fellow Founding Father, advised Warren to be careful the night before his fatal injury. Warren replied he would die in shame if he remained in safety, while other patriots he inspired shed their blood and lives for their cause.

We first learn of Dr. Warren, one of the earliest members of the Sons of Liberty, participating in meetings beginning in 1768. Where patriots gathered, they could always count on Warren appearing or supporting them. He was a leader of the Boston Committee on Safety and Correspondence, which supported the Minutemen and helped plan the Boston Tea Party.

He inspired citizens reminding them of their inheritance from forebears who risked lives crossing the Atlantic Ocean searching for freedom of religion and from oppression. During a March 6, 1775 speech commemorating the Boston Massacre, Warren urged citizens to **"act worthy of yourselves."**

Warren asked Paul Revere and William Dawes to ride on April 18, 1775, to warn Samuel Adams, John Hancock, and the people of Lexington that the British regulars were on the move to arrest them and confiscate all the weapons they found. That order preceded "the shot heard around the world," igniting the Revolutionary War the next day.

The significance of his leadership resulted in his election as President of the Massachusetts Provincial Congress. Joseph Warren's profession as a doctor allowed him to travel and see many people so he set up a spy network at great personal risk to his life and livelihood.

Many identified Dr. Joseph Warren as a Founding Grandfather who led by action, example, and sacrifice, inspiring countless others who followed him. He is also remembered as a Founding Martyr. Dr. Warren deserves our remembrance, honor, and our efforts in preserving the freedom he and his fellow patriots gifted us.

The Founders and following ancestors bought and extended our liberty, never experiencing the pleasure and plenty we too often take for granted. I often remind people, "**Our parents could only dream of what we feel entitled to, and our grandparents couldn't even conceive of it.**" All previous generations encountered, endured, and persevered through more difficult times than current generations.

As Warren exhorted Bostonians, we should remember his words equally every day,

"Our country is in danger, but not to be despaired of. Our enemies are numerous and powerful; but we have many friends, determining to be free, and heaven and earth will aid the resolution. **On you depend the fortunes of America. You are to decide the important question, on which rest the happiness and liberty of millions yet unborn. Act worthy of yourselves.**"

ALEXANDER HAMILTON

"What is the most sacred duty and the greatest source of our security in a Republic? An inviolable respect for the Constitution and Laws."

In case you thought Alexander Hamilton (January 11, 1755 – July 12, 1804) was merely a character in a modern musical, his picture on our ten-dollar bill proves he lived and was a leading Founding Father of The United States.

Few would have predicted the achievements and influence he would wield when he was born on the island now known as Saint Kitts and Nevis in the Caribbean. Many believe he was self-educated very early in his life.

Alexander worked as a bookkeeper at eleven years old when his father abandoned the family. His work impressed others, and they sponsored him to travel to New Jersey and eventually to King's College for formal education.

As independence efforts amplified, Hamilton defended the Boston Tea Party and later added clout to the political debates by authoring papers discussing the issues.

Hamilton's leadership skills resulted in friends helping him earn a commission as a captain in the Continental Army in 1776. His contributions in Trenton the day after Christmas caught the attention of General George Washington, who advanced him as his aide-de-camp and chief secretary.

Alexander's quick study of Washington's habits and methods earned the general's trust, further increasing his reputation as the general's alter-ego.

Hamilton's prestige grew when he served as a delegate to the Constitutional Convention. Hamilton advocated a strong central government and authored at least two-thirds of the 85 Federalist Papers. His writings on the Constitution and public policy continue to influence our government and benefit citizens today.

Hamilton served as the first secretary of the treasury of The United States, establishing principles enabling financial prosperity for Americans and protecting them from abuse by politicians. He promoted a national bank, sound economic principles and warned against the evils of perpetual public debt.

Leaving the cabinet in 1795, Hamilton continued to wield political influence, including establishing the Federalist Party and in the 1800 election.

Alexander Hamilton later founded *The New York Post* newspaper in 1801.

His political disagreements with Vice-President Aaron Burr escalated, hardening both their hearts and resulting in Hamilton's mortal wounding in a duel in 1804.

Hamilton is an excellent example of someone whose birth and early life did not define who he was. His rise in achievements demonstrates the possibilities of success for everyone in America. He was trustworthy, a hard worker, a lifetime learner, and loved his adopted United States, which resulted in his being one of the most significant Founding Fathers.

ALEXANDER HAMILTON QUOTES

"Perseverance in almost any plan is better than fickleness and fluctuation."

"Give all the power to the many, they will oppress the few. Give all the power to the few, they will oppress the many."

"The natural cure for an ill-administration, in a popular or representative constitution, is a change of men."

"When avarice (greed) takes the lead in a state, it is commonly the forerunner of its fall."

"Great Ambition, unchecked by principle, or the love of Glory, is an unruly Tyrant."

"Divisions at home would invite dangers from abroad."

"The nation which can prefer disgrace to danger is prepared for a master and deserves one."

"We must make the best of those ills which cannot be avoided."

ROGER SHERMAN

"The question is, not what rights belong to man, but how they may be most equally and effectually guarded in society."

Fate smiled on a few Founders and patriots, enshrining them into our eternal memory, but there were so many others to whom we owe a debt of thanks for their contributions to our liberty.

One of those is Roger Sherman (April 19, 1721 – July 23, 1793) of Connecticut. He was another unlikely hero who demonstrated that every American has the capacity and opportunity to serve and contribute to the country and fellow citizens more than anyone could imagine.

His family's modest means limited his formal education and placed him on a path as a shoemaker. His father died when Roger was nineteen, requiring him also to manage the small family farm. While apprenticing as a shoemaker, his desire to achieve more ignited his thirst for learning by reading.

Eventually, Roger pursued a legal profession and was admitted to the Bar, beginning a career as a judge and elected official. As the calls for Independence increased, Sherman's activities in Connecticut boosted him into a leadership role. He joined representatives from all thirteen colonies in Philadelphia as a member of the Continental Congress in 1774 and actively participated in that world-changing summer of 1776.

Sherman joined fifty-five other patriots in signing the Declaration of Independence, pledging their "lives, fortunes, and sacred honor." It is hard for us to fully understand their commitment and the suffering the group experienced for the next seven years. His age and experience proved more valuable serving in Congress and on the Committee on Safety rather than in a combat role.

After winning Independence, Sherman continued his public service as a judge.

When calls to revise the Articles of Confederation rose, Sherman was again selected to serve as a delegate to the Constitutional Convention of 1787. Representatives knew the importance of their task of creating a governing document more permanent and successful than the confederation formed after the Revolution.

They began on May 25, 1787, and talked, studied, and deliberated until the thirty-nine delegates endorsed a final document on September 17, which we celebrate as Constitution Day. Though well-documented, it is difficult for us to understand the pressure they experienced and their ability to disagree without being disagreeable in debating every word into the document.

Among the many issues that could have prevented the Constitution's approval was the disagreement between small and large states. Small states wanted a legislative body with equal representation for every state. Larger states wanted a Congress assigning representatives based on each state's population. Neither group would yield to the other, threatening the entire effort.

Finally, Roger Sherman and fellow Connecticut delegate Oliver Ellsworth came up with the idea to create a bi-cameral legislative branch, including the House of Representatives with more members assigned by the population of each state and a Senate where each state would receive two members. Known as the **Connecticut** or **Great Compromise**, delegates adopted it in July. Two more months of intense negotiations and deliberations followed before representatives ratified the Constitution.

Roger Sherman was one of six men who signed the Declaration of Independence *and* the Constitution, making him an essential contributor to the founding of The United States. He and Robert Morris were the only men to sign those two documents, plus The Continental Association and the Articles of Confederation.

Our Constitution remains the longest-serving governing document in the world today, which further testifies to the founders' forethought and the uniqueness of the government they gave us.

Roger Sherman continued his lifelong service to his country, and serves as another example demonstrating it is not where you begin in life that counts but where you finish.

His example also encourages us, as President John F. Kennedy stated, "One person can make a difference, and everyone should try."

Roger Sherman Quotes

"Government is instituted for those who live under it."

"The executive should be able to repel and not commence war."

"If the president alone was vested with the power of appointing all officers and was left to select a council for himself, he woulde be liable to be deceived by flatterers and pretenders to patriotism."

"If you are in the minority, speak, if in the majority, vote."

"Let us live no more to ourselves, but to Him who loved us and gave Himself to die for us."

John Marshall

"Our Constitution is color-blind and neither knows nor tolerates classes among citizens. In respect of civil rights, all citizens are equal before the law. The humblest is the peer of the most powerful."

Though John Marshall (September 24, 1755 – July 6, 1835) significantly impacted the 19th century (and beyond), his accomplishments in the 18th century prepared him for his most significant accomplishment as Chief Justice of the Supreme Court for thirty-plus years.

Marshall was born and raised in a modest log cabin, the oldest of fifteen children. John was good-natured, intelligent, and possessed a good sense of humor. Despite lacking a formal education, his parents encouraged him to learn from a deacon who tutored him in exchange for room and board and also supported his passion for extensive reading.

He enlisted at the same time as his father in the Virginia militia after the battle at Lexington and saw combat in several actions, rising to the rank of Lieutenant.

After leaving the military, Marshall continued his preparation for future greatness by studying law at William and Mary. Following passing the Bar, he was elected to serve in the State Assembly, where he promoted the adoption of the U.S. Constitution. President Adams sent him to France to negotiate an end to French attacks on American shipping. Marshall's leadership ability was evident to many, leading to his election to the House of Representatives, being one of the leaders of the Federalist Party, and his appointment as Secretary of State by President Adams in 1800.

Preparation, study, and Service are always positive ingredients that increase the likelihood of success.

Said differently, Marshall's beliefs can be expressed in the following equation:
Observation + Study + Experience + Service = Preparation to meet future opportunities.

As the 19th century dawned, Marshall's 18th-century endeavors positioned him for an even more significant impact on the people of his time and continuing in our time and beyond.

One of President Adams's last actions was a lame-duck appointment of John Marshall to Chief Justice of the Supreme Court in 1801, where he served until 1835. The most famous case under Marshall was Marbury vs. Madison in 1803, where the court established the principle of judicial review securing the court's right to declare national or state laws unconstitutional.

He presided over more than 1,000 cases writing about half of the opinions himself, demonstrating his leadership in fact and opinion.

In his second most famous case, McCullough vs. Maryland in 1819, Marshall's court struck another blow for Federalism, approving the government's ability to create a national bank as a tool to carry out its powers granted in the Constitution, describing the authority as "implied powers."

As one would expect from a thirty-plus-year tenure in a position competing for power with the executive and legislative branches of government, the court didn't please everyone under Marshall any more than it does today. In the well-known decision of Worcester vs. Georgia, which stated that states could not enact laws on Native American lands, President Andrew Jackson was so upset with the court he declared, "Marshall has made his decision; now let him enforce it."

John Marshall was one of the last living Founders, and his lifetime of service to his country and people not only influences all of us today but is worthy of our study and emulation of a well-lived life.

JOHN MARSHALL QUOTES

"A constitution is framed for ages to come, and is designed to approach immortality as nearly as human institutions can approach it."

"The judicial power does not include a right to change the Constitution."

"The peculiar circumstances of the moment may render a measure more or less wise, but cannot render it more or less constitutional."

"What are the maxims of Democracy? A strict observance of justice and public faith, and a steady adherence to virtue.

"The very essence of civil liberty...consists in the right of every individual to claim protection of the laws, whenever he receives an injury. One of the first duties of government is to afford that protection. – Marbury vs. Madison, 1803

"The power to tax is the power to destroy."

"To listen well is as powerful means of communication and influence as to talk well."

Samuel Chase

"Religion is of general and public concern, and on its support depend in great measure, the peace and good order of government, the safety and happiness of the people."

Samuel Chase's father was a pastor and ensured his only child received a thorough classical education leading to his reading the law and entering the legal profession. Opportunities created by the times and his internal drive led him to lead the kind of life that would leave his mark on his country and its people for generations beyond his time under the sun.

Samuel's (April 17, 1741 – June 19, 1811) public service began at twenty years old in the Provincial Assembly, younger than most elected officials, indicating his community's trust in his character and abilities to serve them. From the beginning, his independent nature and outspokenness stood out from others who were satisfied to avoid ruffling British feathers.

His leadership skills won him a seat in the Continental Congress in 1774 and again in 1775 and 1776. Chase was an early advocate for independence and proudly signed The Declaration of Independence.

In 1778, he returned briefly to private life but reappeared to serve as Chief Justice of the Maryland Supreme Court before President Washington nominated him to The United States Supreme Court.

Samuel Chase's character was impeccable. His honesty, integrity, and Christian walk gained him respect and an admirable reputation with all but those who dealt in bare-knuckle partisan politics.

***

The Founders put aside their human differences by working together despite their disagreements and compromising to achieve the ultimate goal of Independence.

How quickly the Founders reverted to personal opinions and agendas after the founding of the United States illustrates how monumental the independence effort was. The absence of other republics achieving equal success in history is additional proof of American exceptionalism.

Political parties debuted early in America and divided Founders whose singular purpose and efforts were essential to birth our country. Presidents Washington and Adams were both members of the Federalist Party, but President Jefferson's election ushered in the first administration of the Democratic-Republican party. From the beginning, Jefferson took advantage of every opportunity to reduce the power of the judiciary and federal government. He believed judges, including Chase, issued rulings beneficial to the Federalist Party.

***

Finally, President Jefferson persuaded the House of Representatives to impeach Chase in March 1804 for misconduct. In reality, it was because he disagreed with the president, and his court actions were partisan. The House voted on the eight counts in December 1804. The Senate, led by 23 Democratic-Republicans over 9 Federalists, acquitted him on all counts in March 1805. His legal victory could not have occurred if votes had been cast exclusively along party lines, as we often see today. Thankfully, the split party votes indicate that each Senator took the responsibility seriously.

Samuel Chase continues to be the only Supreme Court justice ever impeached. Many see the rebuke of the partisan impeachment as securing the independence of the judicial branch of government.

His impeachment, contentious trial, and acquittal demonstrate the rough and tumble politics of the 21st century's ancestors lived in the 18th century and before. He continued to honorably serve on the Supreme Court until he died in 1811.

Among his legacy, he showed us how to be resolute when unjustifiably attacked for purely political motives. He also demonstrated the nobility that honesty, integrity, character, principle, lifelong learning, and serving others accomplishes.

Samuel Chase was an AmeriCAN worthy of our honor and emulation.

Samuel Chase quotes

"The jury has the right to determine both the law and the facts."

"Summon me, then; I will be the posse commitatus; I will take them to jail."

DR. JOHN WITHERSPOON

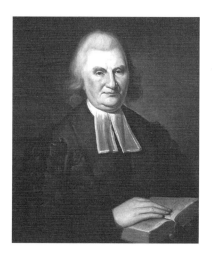

"The future and success of America is not in this Constitution, but in the laws of God upon which this Constitution is founded."

John Witherspoon (February 5, 1723 – November 15, 1794) was born in Scotland to a minister who ensured he received the highest education based on moral and religious principles and hoped he followed his father's ministerial footsteps.

Witherspoon's early adulthood found him earning his divinity degree and, for the next 25 years, establishing a reputation for his pastoral service, wisdom, and theological authorship. John's strong Protestant, nationalist, and republicanism beliefs developed during his ministry in Scotland.

It is impressive that John Witherspoon's reputation crossed the Atlantic, earning him an invitation to come to America to accept the position of President of The College of New Jersey (now Princeton College) in 1768. At the time, its primary purpose was training ministers. Witherspoon's leadership in the church and school raised its stature to educate and prepare leaders for a new country.

His nationalist and republican principles fit into the growing movement for independence. John recognized the increase in British authority over the government and church in America as threats to the people's liberties, as he experienced in Scotland. Never one to ignore public issues, Witherspoon spoke up early and often, adding his voice to the growing patriot movement. He preached sermons and wrote about the diverging British and American interests.

New Jersey citizens esteemed John so highly that he was selected to represent them in the Continental Congress, where he joined fifty-five other signers of The Declaration of Independence. He was the first clergyman to serve in Congress, which he did until 1784.

While some today (who are quick to criticize but short on accomplishments) focus on a singular human imperfection based on twenty-first-century morals, Witherspoon stands tall among America's Founders contributing to our founding principles, government, educational, and spiritual ideals.

John Witherspoon served people as a pastor, college president, statesman, and patriot. Few rival his contributions to our liberty and the gift of freedom we enjoy.

John Witherspoon Quotes

"Those, therefore, who pay no regard to religion and sobriety in the persons whom they send to the legislature of any State are guilty of the greatest absurdity and will soon pay dear for their folly."

"The people in general ought to have regard to the moral character of those whom they invest with authority either in the legislative, executive, or judicial branches."

"Those who wish well to the State ought to choose places of trust men of inward principle, justified by exemplary conversation."

"If your cause is just, you may look with confidence to the Lord and entreat Him to plead it as His own."

"Never rise to speak until you have something to say; and when you have said it, cease."

GEORGE MASON

"I ask, Sir, what is the Militia? It is the whole people. To disarm the people is the best and most effectual way to enslave them."

George Mason (December 11, 1725 – October 7, 1792) was another unique Founding Father as he did not sign either the Declaration of Independence or the Constitution but influenced the individual liberty of ALL Americans past, present, and future through his advocacy of The Bill of Rights.

George was born into a wealthy family but lost his father by drowning when he was ten. Like many other leaders of the period, he received a thorough classical education in a one-on-one environment with contracted teachers and an uncle.

When he was twenty-one, he inherited his father's estate. With it came the obligation and opportunity to impact public policy, which Mason did, holding various offices and serving in the local militia. He actively managed and expanded his business interests, married, and fathered nine children.

Mason's political beliefs and thinking first appeared when he was elected to the Virginia House of Burgesses in 1758. His star steadily ascended as he served on numerous committees, growing his reputation and knowledge.

By the time Britain invoked the Stamp Act in 1765, Mason's philosophy firmly favored colonial rights, and he increasingly communicated his views through his writing and speaking. His response to the Stamp Act advocated eliminating slavery ahead of most leaders of the day.

His most significant impact on all Americans began with his major contribution to the Virginia Constitution and Declaration of Rights in 1776. His authorship drew on predecessors back to the Magna Carta. Mason's writing and political efforts focused on individual rights, which eventually resulted in adding the Bill of Rights to the United States Constitution.

Mason was an active delegate to the Constitutional Convention. Still, his conviction toward the Bill of Rights was so absolute that he was one of three delegates to vote against adopting the final version without its inclusion. Persistent efforts by Mason and others led to the Bill of Rights ratification in 1791.

George Mason was underappreciated in his day and still is today. He deserves our thanks and appreciation every day when we breathe the air of freedom, exercise our rights to speak, worship, protect our families, and are protected against government overreach.

GEORGE MASON QUOTES

"The laws of nature are the laws of God, whose authority can be superseded by no power on earth."

"How easy it is to persuade men to sign anything by which they can't be affected."

"There is a passion natural to the mind of man, especially a free man, which renders him impatient of restraint."

"Our All is at Stake, and the little Conveniences and Comforts of Life, when set in Competition with our Liberty, ought to be rejected not with Reluctance but with Pleasure."

"In all our associations; in all our agreements let us never lose sight of this fundamental maxim – that all power was originally lodged in, and consequently is derived from, the people."

"Every society, all government, and every kind of civil compact therefore, is or ought to be, calculated for the general good and safety of the community."

"A few years' experience will convince us that those things which at the time they happened we regarded as our greatest misfortunes have proved our greatest blessings."

"The freedom of the press is one of the great bulwarks of liberty, and can never be restrained but by despotic governments."

"Those gentlemen, who will be elected Senators, will fix themselves in the federal town, and become citizens of that town more than of your state."

Robert Morris

"I am not one of those politicians that run testy when my own plans are not adopted. I think it is the duty of a good citizen to follow when he cannot lead." He also stated, "While I do not wish to see my countrymen die on the field of battle nor do I wish to see them live in tyranny."

One of the fascinating facts about the Founders is how unique each individual and their contributions were to successfully establish the longest-lasting and most prosperous Constitutional Republic in history. For believers, the assembly of the people and the timing of the independence movement prove God's Providence, Grace, Mercy, and Blessing upon our land and people. Non-believers attribute events differently.

Robert Morris (January 20, 1734 - May 8, 1806) exemplified the uniqueness of each Founder. He was **one of two men (joining Roger Sherman) who signed the Declaration of Independence, Articles of Confederation, and the Constitution of The United States, cementing his inclusion as a Founding Father.**

Known as the "Financier of the American Revolution," his story proves truth is stranger than fiction.

Robert was born in England and came to America at thirteen years old. Formal education did not interest him, and he entered an apprenticeship at fifteen in a counting room, which tapped and grew his expertise with numbers and money. At twenty-one years old, he partnered in launching an export business and began his path to wealth.

Content in operating his business affairs, the shots at Lexington and Concord aroused his interest and commitment to independent public affairs. Soon after, he was elected to the Pennsylvania legislature and a delegate to the Congress. His financial expertise stood out, and he was assigned to planning and paying for the war effort.

When Washington faced the loss of much of the Army at the end of their enlistment in 1776, he asked Morris to send money to pay bonuses for troops to re-enlist. Robert Morris answered the call then, and every other time a crisis appeared and loaned ten thousand dollars for the troops. Robert's gift of finding money throughout the conflict proved invaluable, though unseen by the public, partially explaining his lack of recognition.

In 1781, he was called upon to create a bank to finance the war, essentially serving as Secretary of the Treasury. Later in the year, his personal efforts to secure financial backing of the Army enabled Washington to win the last major battle of the war at Yorktown, leading to the Treaty of Paris in 1783 and independence!

Morris served as Superintendent of Finance for the new government, in the Pennsylvania legislature, and U.S. Senate after the war before leaving public life. His financial assistance of the war, and private setbacks led him to spend three years in debtor's prison before being released to breathe the free air he participated in providing others.

***

It is generally easy to find quotes from public figures and politicians because they tend to speak more often than they act, but Robert Morris is the exception. Finding quotes for him is a supreme challenge, but seeing his irreplaceable actions that contributed to victory in the Revolutionary War is as easy as normal breathing.

If it is difficult to locate his comments, the following statement from one of his contemporaries adds value to composing his profile.

"Robert Morris (Pennsylvania) is a merchant of great eminence and wealth; an able Financier, and a worthy patriot. He has an understanding equal to any public object and possesses an energy of mind that few Men can boast of. Although he is not learned, yet he is as great as those who are. I am told that when he speaks in the Assembly of Pennsylvania, that he bears down all before him. **What could have been his reason for not Speaking in the Convention I know not, but he never once spoke on any point.** This Gentleman is about 50 years old." — **Character Sketches of Delegates to the Federal Convention by William Pierce (1787)**

Robert Morris's behind-the-scenes leadership in finance was essential to independence and the freedoms we enjoy today. His limited public exposure and later setbacks produce a mixed picture of his life, as most of us would experience.

Regardless of his imperfections, he is worthy of our admiration and appreciation, for without his actions, we may not enjoy the country we inherited.

CHARLES CARROLL OF CARROLLTON

"I do hereby recommend to the present and future generations the principles of that important document as the best earthly inheritance their ancestors could bequeath to them."

Courage! We cannot remember or appreciate enough the courage of all 56 signers of The Declaration of Independence. Charles Carroll (September 20, 1737 - November 14, 1832) put an additional portion of his courage in writing when he added his name.

He was the only Roman Catholic in a time of majority protestant rule to sign and was the last surviving signer of the Declaration of Independence. Roman Catholics were limited in running for public office in his early years, yet that discrimination and its aftermath did not discourage Carroll from participating in public affairs.

He was initially educated at a Jesuit preparatory school when he was eight. From when he was eleven years old until he was twenty-eight years old, he studied in France and London, earning his law degree and advanced education.

His return to Maryland in 1765 occurred as the Stamp Act was instituted, and Charles quickly joined the patriot effort. He authored commentaries against implementing British laws without the colonists' consent under the pen name "The First Citizen," gaining a growing audience across an expanding area.

Once he was revealed as "The First Citizen," people encouraged him to increase his participation in public affairs. He was appointed to the Committee of Safety of Maryland, elected to the state assembly, and appointed to serve with Franklin and Chase as delegates to Canada. He was also elected a delegate to the Continental Congress.

Ironically, he arrived in Philadelphia too late to vote for independence but in time to sign the document. Anti-Catholic delegates reportedly scolded him after signing his name, saying many were named Charles Carroll, and he would easily hide among them to elude the British. He alone then added his hometown to his signature, famously signing "Charles Carroll of Carrollton."

When asked why he signed the document uniquely, he reportedly said, "They cannot mistake me now!"* Each signer's signature made them traitors to the British government, subject to the death penalty. Telling the authorities where they could locate him sounds more like a twenty-first-century "in your face" comment than something gentlemen would do in the eighteenth century.

As reportedly one of the wealthiest men in the colonies, Carroll had more to lose outside his life than the other signers. John Hancock, who used his vast wealth to finance patriot needs, is supposed to have passed the pen to Carroll after affixing his extra-large signature on the Declaration, realizing the example he would add for the other delegates and citizens.

Carroll served his state and country during and after the war for many years in various capacities, including the Continental Congress, Maryland State Senate, and as a United States Senator. He retired from public life at sixty-four years old, and especially after Jefferson and Adams passed, enjoyed the role of Grand Old Patriot.

Charles Carroll of Carrollton lived what President Theodore Roosevelt later advocated when he said, "Do what you can, with what you have, where you're at." It is still good advice for each of us today.

CHARLES CARROLL OF CARROLLTON QUOTES

"Grateful to Almighty God for the blessings which, through Jesus Christ Our Lord, He had conferred on my beloved country in her emancipation and on myself in permitting me, under circumstances of mercy, to live to the age of 89 years and to survive the fiftieth year of independence, adopted by Congress on the 4th of July 1776..."

"Without morals a republic cannot subsist any length of time; they therefore who are decrying the Christian religion, whose morality is so sublime and pure (and) which insures to the good eternal happiness, are undermining the solid foundation of morals, the best security for the duration of free governments."

* Lossing, B.J., *Lives of the Signers of the Declaration of Independence*, originally published 1848, and reprinted by WallBuilders Press in 1995, page 160.

Patriots

The Spirit of '76 by Archibald Willard – 1875

"In the beginning of a change, the patriot is a scarce man, and brave and hated and scorned. When his cause succeeds the timid join him, for then it costs nothing to be a patriot."

—Mark Twain

"We fight, get beat, rise, and fight again."

—General Nathanael Greene, right before
the US victory in Yorktown, May 1781

"To restore harmony, to render us again one people acting as one nation should be the object of every man really a patriot."

—Thomas Jefferson

John Paul Jones

"Surrender? I have not yet begun to fight!"

These are the words John Paul Jones (July 6, 1747 – July 18, 1792) spoke on September 23, 1779, when the British captain of the Serapis asked Jones if he wanted to surrender while commanding the Bonhomme Richard in an hours-long fight. Both vessels severely damaged each other and suffered high casualties.

No one dreamed John Paul, his birth name, born in Scotland, would become a naval legend. He was another American who achieved more than anyone suspected because he applied his can-do spirit to the opportunity America allowed him.

He began his career at sea as a cabin boy when he was 12 years old and steadily progressed until he owned his ship. After a mutiny on board the vessel where the ringleader was killed, John

Paul escaped the West Indies islands and became John Paul Jones to avoid future encounters with the legal system.

When the Revolution began, Jones secured a commission in the Continental Navy and discovered many were given choice commands because of their political connections over his superior sea experience. Because he came from humble beginnings, he argued positions should be assigned on merit, which opened doors of opportunities in the true American spirit.

Great Britain dominated the seas, and the Continental Navy barely existed. Few imagined anyone could defeat the British Navy. The adversity Jones overcame with the most famous American naval quote ever stated proved true when the British surrendered, and Jones transferred command to the Serapis as the Bonhomme Richard sank.

Jones promoted offensive naval tactics and strategies of utilizing the French Navy against the British to support Continental troops. He set high ideals combined with advanced education, realizing the result would be the most professional Navy in the world.

After the war, Jones served in Denmark and Russia and faded from view in America. While waiting for additional opportunities to help others, he died and was buried in Paris, honored by the French but forgotten by most Americans.

More than 100 years later, Civil War general Horace Porter made it his personal mission to locate John Paul Jones's body and return it for reburial and the honor it deserved in America. After six long years and a winding trail, Porter succeeded. Our country reburied Jones in a tomb at the United States Naval Academy in Annapolis, Maryland, where he continues to be honored.

Jones was imperfect, as we all are. Still, while others focused only on self-promotion or winning the Revolution, he envisioned a navy for the United States superior to any in the world. He is credited by many as the founder of the United States Navy.

His efforts in establishing the Navy contributed to the founding of the United States, which continues to protect our freedom today.

JOHN PAUL JONES QUOTES

"Since liberty hath chosen America as her last asylum every effort to protect and cherish her is noble and will be rewarded with the thanks of future ages."

"I would lay down my life for America, but I cannot trifle with my Honor."

"It is true that I must run a great risk; no gallant action was ever accomplished without danger."

"It seems to be a law of nature, inflexible and inexorable, that those who will not risk cannot win."

"If fear is cultivated it will become stronger, if faith is cultivated it will achieve mastery."

"Where men of fine feeling are connected there is seldom misunderstanding."

"I will have no connection with any ship that does not sail fast, for I intend to go into harm's way."

"He who will not risk cannot win."

Anna Smith Strong

honoringourpatriots.dar.org

"It's revenge I'm after, and I'll see it done."

The American Revolution produced a generation of strong men and also many tough women, including Anna Smith Strong (April 14, 1740- August 12, 1812), who lived a life worthy of her name. They are often overlooked, but if not for their direct efforts in supporting the Army and community, victory would have been impossible. It is the same in any war.

Anna was born into a wealthy family, many of whom were Tories (British sympathizers). She married at 20 and eventually had ten children.

Anna's husband, Selah, was the local judge and a minuteman. The British constantly harassed him before placing him on the prison ship Jersey in New York harbor in 1778. Conditions were miserable on those ships, and more than 11,000 Americans died on them during the war. Knowing the suffering Selah and others experienced inspired Anna to seek revenge.

With her childhood friends, Anna joined the Culper spy ring. They took great personal risk watching the British Army for General George Washington; twenty-one-year-old Nathan Hale was hung in 1776 without a trial when he was arrested in New York for spying.

Anna's job was primarily passing signals between the other spies, often using her laundry line to do so. Before dryer machines, which we take for granted today, people hung washed clothes on wire or rope lines outside to dry under the sun and wind. The laundry code Anna used included hanging a black petticoat to signal messages were ready to be picked up and adding handkerchiefs to communicate where the information was located.

Anna begged the British to release Selah, and they eventually did so. He left Long Island and took their younger children to Connecticut. She remained in Setauket, Long Island, throughout the war, continuing her participation in the spy ring.

George Washington relied on the Culper ring for intelligence, enabling him to produce strategies and tactics to win the war and secure liberty for Americans.

Anna was the unlikeliest of spies, but like so many other women she helped where she was in the way she could, assuming great personal risk and sacrificing her own comfort without any expectation of notice or appreciation.

Anna and the other spies' contributions to winning the war and our freedom was their reward. Even after the war concluded, they never sought attention or profit from their actions.

Anna and Selah returned to their Setauket home, had their 10th child, and lived the remainder of their lives as ordinary but free Americans.

The discovery of a chest of old letters in 1939 revealed the Culper spy ring. The long secrecy of the spies indicates their close personal bonds. This late discovery explains why images of her are unavailable or undiscovered. In our day of people jumping up and demanding recognition of the slightest accomplishment, Anna and the members of Culper are refreshing examples of love of country and selfless sacrifice.

PAUL REVERE

"No matter what you do, you'll never run away from you."

We almost exclusively remember Paul Revere (January 1, 1735 – May 10, 1818) because of his famous ride, but he deserves our remembrance for much more.

Paul's father passed along his silversmith trade to Paul, but like so many others, Paul became a more substantial citizen than in that profession alone. Too often, we perceive people based on what we know about them instead of contemplating their whole story, and they pigeonhole us the same way based on their limited knowledge of our activities.

Paul's education and ability to read and reason enabled him to interact and equally serve the working and intellectual classes in his business efforts. As discussions of British oppression advanced, his leadership role increased, and he served as a salesman for liberty and independence.

While he practiced his craft, Paul actively participated in building the independence movement. Revere served patriots by observing British activities while conducting his business. He donned an Indian disguise as a Son of Liberty, throwing tea into Boston Harbor in 1773, showing he was not only a man of talk but action also.

Paul became the chief rider for the Boston Committees of Safety and Correspondence, which may be one reason he was the most famous messenger on April 18, 1775. He risked life and limb to warn Sam Adams, John Hancock, and Lexington and Concord communities that "the regulars are out." Everyone in America at that time was British, which is why the redcoat soldiers were called "regulars." After securing our new nation, Americans quickly changed the alarm Revere and William Dawes cried out to, "The British are coming," further signifying our independence and new country.

Their warnings enabled minutemen to assemble ahead of troops arriving in Lexington, resulting in "the shot heard round the world" on April 19, 1775. Thus, talk of a revolution to gain independence ended, and an eight-year-long painful war began.

When I was in public school, we had history and civics classes where we learned and memorized the introduction to Longfellow's famous poem about Paul Revere's ride, which cemented his reputation nationally.

PAUL REVERE'S RIDE
by Henry Wadsworth Longfellow
Published in 1861

Listen, my children, and you shall hear
Of the midnight ride of Paul Revere,
On April 18th, in Seventy-five;
Hardly a man is now alive
Who remembers that famous day and year?

During the war, Revere's industrial efforts contributed needed materials, including gunpowder and cannon, and printed Continental currency. Paul served in the militia, including commanding Castle William in Boston Harbor.

Liberty secured, Paul continued serving his community and country as a free citizen. His two marriages produced sixteen children.

Known to many as a patriot and silversmith, Paul also was an entrepreneur, industrial manufacturer, community leader, volunteer, husband, and father. Americans past, present, and future benefit from his life and actions because he matured into a multi-talented leader.

In all of Revere's achievements, he lived a life worthy of example as a servant leader.

MOLLY PITCHER

MOLLIE PITCHER TAKING HER HUSBAND'S PLACE AFTER HE FELL AT THE BATTLE OF MONMOUTH

"If that cannonball were just a little higher, it would have carried off something more important than a petticoat."

Many women contributed to the Continental Army and the Revolutionary War effort. Some believe Molly Pitcher was a compilation of multiple ladies and their invaluable efforts.

Others believe Mary Ludwig (October 13, 1754 – January 22, 1832), who married William Hays, was Molly. Her family was one of modest means, which most likely limited her formal education.

Like countless other wives, she followed William when he went to war and contributed in various ways to patriot efforts, including bringing water to the troops during the fighting. Many believe this is where she earned her nickname, Molly Pitcher.

These women served their families and their country with little thanks or recognition.

Molly manned a cannon when William was injured during the Battle of Monmouth (1778). Some report George Washington noticed her action and promoted her to a non-commissioned officer revising her nickname to Sergeant Molly. She continued in the Army until the war's end. She is called America's First Heroine.

The National Archives contains a statement from Joseph Plumb Martin that a cannonball went between her legs during the battle, only damaging her petticoat. He quoted her saying, "If that cannonball were a little higher, it would have carried away something else." If true, it would reveal her composure and sense of humor.

As typical by so many of our forebears, her servant's heart led to a lifetime of contributions to her fellow citizens. Mary served the public working in the state legislature for many years and was eventually awarded a veteran's pension.

***

Another possible contender as Molly Pitcher was Margaret Corbin, who followed her husband, John, to war. She wore a uniform and saw combat when John was injured. Margaret was later wounded and captured by the British. Eventually, she was released and served as a guard at West Point.

***

Whether Molly was Mary, Margaret, another woman, or a compilation of several ladies, no one argues that women contributed and sacrificed to our independence in many ways.

They deserve our honor, appreciation, and inclusion in a special place in our memory as heroes who assisted in building the country we are blessed to live in.

CHRISTOPHER SEIDER (SNIDER)

A Young Patriot and the First Casualty of the American Revolution

Christopher Seider (or Snider) (1758 – February 22, 1770) was only eleven years old but already possessed the soul of a patriot in 1770. He was one of many Liberty Boys who joined the Sons of Liberty activities.

Early in 1770, Bostonians' frustration with their treatment from England reached a boiling point. The unequal treatment of loyalists and patriots increased tensions and divided the people.

Increased taxes and a large presence of British troops led to troops receiving insults and an increasing number of physical attacks. Ordinary citizens protested publicly in growing numbers and noise.

On February 22, a protest of a loyalist importing British goods instead of buying from local colonists grew out of hand. Ebenezer Richardson, a British customs officer, attempted to break up the demonstration but only increased the anger toward him. Protesters followed his attempt to escape as he found safety in a house.

As the pressure from the crowd's grievance grew, Richardson fired a warning shot, attempting to disburse them. Some in the assembly ran, and others ducked at the sound of the rifle.

Unknowingly and unintentionally, the bullet struck Christopher Seider (Snider). He crumpled to the ground, and his blood flowed into the road. Shocked to see Christopher on the street, Sons of Liberty members raced to his side. No prayer or medical care of that day changed the outcome of the rifle shot, and Christopher's soul had already ascended into eternity.

News spread through the city of the atrocity, and anger against the British grew. More than 1,000 people attended Christopher's funeral, which was held at the famous Liberty Tree. Famed poet Phillis Wheatley memorialized Christopher with a poem.

Less than two weeks later, the Boston Massacre would occur on March 5, further infuriating the citizens of Boston. Five citizens were killed in the street following an initial shot from a British soldier. Seider and those killed in the Boston Massacre were buried together, and their sacrifice motivated the Sons of Liberty as they planned and carried out the Boston Tea Party on December 16, 1773, continuing the escalation of discontent leading to the Revolutionary War.

Richardson would be tried and convicted of manslaughter but would spend less time imprisoned than the people desired. Wisely, he left for England to escape an unhappy public.

It is never too soon to pursue our dreams or exercise our beliefs, and we will not know what we may accomplish if we do not act. Who would think an eleven-year-old boy could inspire people beyond his lifetime?

While Christopher lost his life exercising his beliefs, the example of his actions benefitting Americans continues for those grateful to our Founding Fathers and patriots.

NATHAN HALE

Bound and awaiting execution

"*I only regret I have but one life to give my country,*"

Young Nathan Hale is said to have spoken these last words before the British hung him as a spy.

***

Heroes come in all forms, and Nathan Hale (June 6, 1755 - September 22, 1776) earned immortality because of his bravery as a twenty-one-year-old captain and secret agent for General George Washington and the Army of American Patriots.

After the Battle of Long Island (or Brooklyn Heights) in August 1776, the Continental Army escaped across the East River into Manhattan. New York was crucial to winning independence, but Washington didn't know how the British would follow up their victory. Losing New York was one thing, but losing the Army would end the war.

Washington needed intelligence on British plans and activities, and Hale volunteered to obtain it, though he had no experience, and the job included the highest risk. His grit was mightier than his qualifications. He almost completed his mission when a relative betrayed him and turned him into the British Army, who quickly captured him.

The rules of war then and now call for quickly executing spies captured out of recognized military uniforms.

Hale knew the risk when he volunteered and recognized mercy or a do-over would not excuse his fate. General Sir William Howe sentenced him to hang without a trial or appeal within hours.

Approaching his transition to eternity, observers noted his calm and dignity. His life began and ended, thinking of serving causes larger than himself and others.

As the soldiers placed the noose around his neck, Hale quoted the play *Cato: A Tragedy* as his last words before the stool was kicked out from under him, resulting' in his hanging. The quote from the play follows:

> *How beautiful is death, when earned by virtue!*
> *Who would not be that youth! What pity is it*
> *That we can die but once to serve our country.*

When schools taught American history, we learned of Hale's courageous statement as, "*I only regret I have but one life to give my country.*" Today, few schools educate students about his extraordinary service and example.

Nathan Hale's too-short life was one of honor, achievement, and promise for other great things. His family emphasized education, hard work, and religious virtue. He enrolled in Yale at fourteen years of age and graduated at eighteen, which is unheard of in current times.

His sacrifice and courage immortalized him beyond any dream or desire of his. He is an outstanding example for all who love their country and seeks to contribute to it and its citizen's prosperity.

NATHAN HALE QUOTE

"I am not influenced by the expectation or pecuniary reward. I wish to be useful, and every kind of service for the public good becomes honorable by being necessary."

Benjamin Tallmadge

"Precisely similar, and similar will be your fate." Tallmadge speaking of Nathan Hale to Major John Andre before his trial and execution.

General George Washington knew the importance of accurate intelligence from the beginning of the Revolutionary War. His initial effort failed, resulting in twenty-one-year-old Lieutenant Nathan Hale's hanging. Hale's sacrifice hurt Washington but did not deter his intelligence gathering or how he would handle a future British spy after his famous effort to capture Washington.

***

The British commanded New York City, dividing the colonies and threatening the independence movement. In 1778, Washington ordered Major Benjamin Tallmadge (February 25, 1754 - March 7, 1835) to create a spy ring in the New York area because it housed British headquarters and its geographic importance.

We've already recognized Anna Strong Smith, who was a member of the Culper Spy Ring, as it was named. I include Tallmadge in this work because of his extraordinary courage to enter the spying business after his friend Nathan Hale's hanging, which was a fate he risked for himself.

Tallmadge recruited other friends whose record of supplying Washington invaluable information and remaining unknown significantly aided the patriot war effort. It speaks highly of Tallmadge's leadership and the team they operated for five years without capture, and to this day, member 355's identity is unknown except that it was a woman.

The ring operated day-in and day-out right under the noses of the British Army. They used available technology to their advantage, including invisible ink and a cipher system utilizing three-digit codes. They communicated messages via dead drops and enclosed them within Tory messages.

***

Tallmadge's early life gave no hint of his future spymaster adventures but was similar to many AmeriCANS of that period. His minister father tutored him before he went to Yale and befriended Nathan Hale. Upon graduation, he began a teaching career interrupted by the independence movement.

Benjamin joined the militia in 1776 and transferred to the Continental Army in 1777, where he fought in several battles.

He quickly rose in the ranks, demonstrating his admirable performance and potential for advanced leadership, as indicated by Washington's selection of him to lead the intelligence operation.

Ironically, Tallmadge was tasked to escort Major John Andre for eight days, leading to his execution for spying, turning Benedict Arnold, and the failed plan to capture West Point and General Washington. Tallmadge's quote above was a reply to Andre's disbelief he would be executed but would be traded for another prisoner. How ironic the connection between Tallmadge and both Andre and Nathan Hale!

After the war, Tallmadge operated a retail store, speculated on land, was a postmaster and a bank president, and served as a U.S. Congressman.

Like so many other successful leaders, Tallmadge lived a life of serving others and contributing to the betterment of America for future generations.

BENJAMIN TALLMADGE QUOTE

"The few quotes attributed to Tallmadge prove he was a man of action rather than words."

"Gen. Washington having recrossed the Schuylkill, determined, on the 16th of September, again to meet Gen. Howe in the field of battle. The arrangements were made and the advance parties had already commenced firing, when there came on a violent shower of rain, which unfitted both armies for action."

—Benjamin Tallmadge,
*Washington's Spymaster: Memoir of
Colonel Benjamin Tallmadge*

Betsy Ross

"Our hearts aching, our prayers praying, our flags waving, never forget."

No one would have suspected that Elizabeth Griscom would have been the most famous of the eighteen kids in her family, much less achieve fame long beyond her lifetime.

As a young lady, her father apprenticed her as an upholsterer and seamstress, where she met and married John Ross, another apprentice. Called Betsy Ross (January 1, 1752 - January 30, 1836) by her friends, she and John opened their own shop in Philadelphia.

John joined the Continental Army and was killed soon after that. Betsy continued her business, married again in 1777, and was quickly widowed again, losing another husband to the war.

In 1783, she married John Claypool and had five more children. Claypool, her daughters, granddaughters, and nieces worked with Betsy over the next fifty years.

Betsy is recognized as making the first stars and stripes flag at the request of General George Washington based on a paper her grandson, George Canby, presented in 1870. He established his claim on his recollections of talking with his grandmother and family member stories, Betsy being in the right place at the right time, and her lifetime and volume of flag making, which one would expect someone with that accomplishment to achieve.

Washington did commission a new flag design in 1776, which included red and white stripes and thirteen stars on a field of blue. The stars were five-pointed, which departed from traditional six-pointed stars. Francis Hopkinson, a member of the Continental Congress, claimed the five-point design as did others for Betsy Ross. Her claim included the fact the five-pointed star is easier to make. The Continental Congress adopted the "Betsy Ross" flag on June 14, 1777, as the first official flag for the United States.

Today's American flag is the 27th version, resulting in the addition of thirty-seven additional states and other minor modifications. The last revision to the flag occurred on July 4, 1960, with the addition of Hawaii as the fiftieth state in the union.

There is no dispute Betsy made many flags during her career, including American, military, and others, for the next fifty years.

Whether she recognized the impact of her contributions to the independence effort, it appears she was so busy taking care of her business and family that she disregarded thumping her chest, claiming any credit for herself. Humility and self-sacrifice for a cause much more significant than self was typical during the Revolutionary period and would serve us well today.

***

Our flag means something to everyone who sees it and should signify even more to EVERY American!

When we look at the flag in the United States, it means one thing. When we see our flag flying while we are in a foreign land, it means so much more: safety, belonging, and liberty.

I thank God we are a free and independent people, citizens who consent to be governed instead of subjects controlled by the state. I thank God for everyone who has sacrificed and served, some paying their last full measure for our liberty. Recognizing all who contributed to creating the most free and prosperous country in the history of the world should instill pride in our hearts and a desire to add our efforts to repay their favor to future generations.

There is a time to protest, but when the flag is posted and the anthem is played, everyone should stand in respect of it!

***

I am thankful for a young seamstress whose work for the Revolutionary War effort earned her a modest living during her life but immortal fame beyond her days. Oh, how we all have, do, and will benefit!

BETSY ROSS QUOTE

"Stars on a field of blue; one for each colony; bars of red, for the blood of sacrifice; on a ground of white for love and peace."

MARY KATHERINE GODDARD

May be a portrait of actress Anne Brunton Merry (1769–1808)
or Mary Katharine Goddard (1738–1816).

*"What think ye of Congress now? That day. . . evidenced
that Americans would rather die than live slaves!"*
—Published in the *Maryland Journal*
April, 1775 after Lexington and Concord

We recognize and honor the 56 men who risked their
"lives, fortunes, and sacred honor" signing the Declaration of
Independence in 1776. Still, very few know of the woman patriot
who exposed herself to the same risk by printing the document
with her name on it also.

Mary Katherine Goddard (June 16, 1738 – August 12, 1816) was an undeservingly unknown brave patriot whose contributions to the Revolutionary War and our liberty deserves our admiration and honor.

Her mother taught her reading, math, science, and classical languages at a time girls were not routinely afforded the opportunity of eduction. Little did anyone know the benefit of her education to Americans during the founding, today, and for the future.

Mary's father and brother operated printing and postal businesses. Her father's death and brother's departure for other endeavors resulted in Mary managing *The Maryland Journal* and soon adding the title of Postmaster of Baltimore to her duties in 1775. She was the first woman to do so.

Mary's pioneering milestones grew into her destiny as the independence movement gained momentum rapidly.

She printed stories on British and patriot activities, advocated for women doing their part wherever they could, and twice published Thomas Paine's *Common Sense*, almanacs, and other jobs.

On January 18, 1777, Mary risked everything printing the first copy of *The Declaration of Independence* with the signer's names included. She typically published her name on all documents as "M.K. Goddard." On The Declaration, she printed her name entirely at the bottom as "Baltimore, In Maryland: Printed by Mary Katherine Goddard." Attaching her name to the most critical piece of paper in American history, added her name to King George's list of traitors to the crown. She risked as much as Hancock Washington, Franklin, and the other signers and simultaneously struck a blow for women's rights and abilities. Her document is known as the *Goddard Broadside.*

Mary was a faithful patriot and continued her printing business until 1784 when a disagreement with her brother led to her exit. She served as Baltimore's postmaster until 1789 when political forces repaid her good deeds by terminating her service.

Despite appealing the loss of her job, she avoided making issues, news, or editorials, which resulted in minimal information about her existence today.

She quietly continued operating her bookstore and printing business for several more years, like so many others who returned to their pre-war lives without asking or expecting any recognition for their varied contributions to winning Independence!

Mary Katherine's success and essential contributions to our liberty could not have occurred without her education, her family's prior work in printing and postal affairs, and Providence, which placed her in the right place at the right time.

First-century Roman Philosopher Seneca said, "Preparation is when luck meets opportunity." Thomas Jefferson believed in luck and stated, I'm a greater believer in luck, and I find the harder I work, the more I have of it. Mary Katherine Goddard prepared, worked hard, and placed herself in positions of service.

More citizens than the signers, Continental Congress, and soldiers risked their lives and sacrificed any pleasures and privileges they may have had for our benefit. It is our obligation to honor their gift by giving it to future generations and educating them on the unique value they inherited and their responsibility to uphold it.

BILLY LEE

Billy Lee (1750 – 1810) is an excellent example demonstrating that it isn't the number or size of our accomplishments that matter but in making the most of the opportunities we are afforded to serve others. We can never know the totality of the impact of our actions.

It is easy to recognize and celebrate AmeriCANS who earned fame during their lifetime, for many of their deeds are easily visible.

However, AmeriCANS come from all races, ages, genders, and times in history, serving others during their lives and influencing many more in the following generations.

Billy Lee was an individual few know about, but who may have had a more significant impact on America and us than we will ever know. Like so many millions of others, Billy Lee is easy to overlook if we only see him with our eyes.

His faithful service to and protection of George Washington as a valet and personal assistant provided His Excellency peace of mind and eased his burden of command throughout the Revolutionary War. His place alongside Washington through thick and thin at Valley Forge, in battles, and other locations enabled him to lighten the pressure of leadership.

Also, what things might he have prevented that put Washington in a position to save the Revolution?

We don't know his full impact or those he influenced during his life, but George Washington's actions express his appreciation and respect for Billy.

Billy was the only enslaved person freed by name in George Washington's will, providing him a pension and home at Mt. Vernon for the rest of his life and where he is buried after his years of faithful service.

Billy's selfless service illustrates we should help who we can, where we can, and how we can.

Everyone who builds, serves, uplifts others, and leaves our country better than they entered is an AmeriCAN.

Any of us during our lives may impact others' lives and influence future generations through our actions, and any improvement, regardless of size, is essential.

President Theodore Roosevelt stated, "Do what you can, with what you have, where you are at." Serving others where we are, improving ourselves to increase our influence, and persisting until our last breath ensures maximizing our days on this earth and the future.

What will we do with our opportunities?

CAPTAIN JOHN PARKER

Henry Hudson Kitson's
The Lexington Minuteman statue (1900)

"Stand your ground. Don't fire unless fired upon, but if they mean to have a war, let it begin here!"

History is full of heroes whose military exploits receive our honor to this day and who parlayed their noble actions into political and business power and success. George Washington, Andrew Jackson, Ulysses S. Grant, Theodore Roosevelt, and Dwight Eisenhower were five of the nine presidents who led the United States after demonstrating their leadership through distinguished military service. Some were citizen soldiers, and others were professional.

The earliest tradition of citizen soldiers began before the United States was founded, with citizens serving in their local militia, defending their communities against all threats, human and natural.

***

Little is known of the early life of John Parker (July 13, 1729 – September 17, 1775). He was born and lived in Lexington, Massachusetts. His family and upbringing gave no reason for people to expect his exemplary leadership or ability to meet a test that changed history.

Although he farmed and was a blacksmith by trade, Parker's experience in the French and Indian War probably led to his election as the Lexington Militia's captain and leader. In early 1775, he suffered from tuberculosis, which would end his life five short months later.

***

We never know when our destiny will appear before us. When it does, will we face it and fulfill our call, or blink, avoiding the opportunity and limiting our lives' fulfillment?

British Prime Minister Benjamin Disraeli said, "The great secret in life is for man to be ready when his opportunity comes."

***

John Parker and the militia in Lexington gathered early in the morning of April 19, 1775, on the Common, wondering what would be asked of them that day. As Paul Revere warned them, the British regulars were out, but what would happen? Would the soldiers come to Lexington? Would they show up in force? If the British appeared, the Lexington men would face overwhelming odds against the most powerful Army in the world. Surely, they would not fight the British? Confusion reigned, which added worry to everyone's thoughts. Seventy-seven men waited in the dark to see what their destiny would be that day.

Lexington was not the objective of the British Army that day, but it stood on the path to achieving its mission to seize John Hancock, John Adams, and the arms and ammunition at Concord, six miles away.

Just before sunrise, the sound of drums, fifes, and marching men filled the air. The militiamen knew it would not be long before the unknown became known. Now the first troops of 700 British soldiers appeared. Tensions rose, and the Lexington men admirably faced their call of duty, deferring their fear to protect their community.

Captain Parker is said to have stated, "Stand your ground. Don't fire unless fired upon, but if they mean to have a war, let it begin here!"

To this day, no one knows who fired "the shot heard round the world" that morning as the sun greeted Lexington. Order vanished as both sides fired upon each other moving to gain what advantage they could locate. When fighting ceased, eight Lexington men lay dead, and one British soldier was wounded.

John Parker's leadership at Lexington inspired his men to stand their ground, act courageously, demonstrate poise under pressure, and fulfill their responsibility to their community and the colonies.

On to Concord, the British advanced, where they met musket fire by local citizens going and returning all the way to Boston. Approximately 300 British were killed or wounded, and 93 colonists met the same fate.

***

Captain Parker and his men later fought in the Siege of Boston before he died in September.

His leadership April 19th, and until tuberculosis cut it short, his life and service will be remembered for their example and selfless servant leadership to Lexington and beyond to the 13 colonies and the United States as long as people remember and celebrate their independence.

***

The Lexington Minuteman statue (1900) by Henry Hudson Kitson represents all the minutemen when sculpted, but many identify today as symbolizing Captain Parker

HENRY KNOX

"The eyes of all America are upon us, as we play our part posterity will bless or curse us."

General Henry Knox (July 25, 1750 – October 25, 1806) illustrates that it is not where you start in life but where you finish that counts. Unlike so many notables from the Revolutionary period, Henry was not born into a prominent home and did not receive a top-notch education.

In fact, Knox dropped out of school at nine years old to work in a bookstore. By the time he was twenty-one years old, he owned his own store.

Henry Knox found himself a peacekeeper at the Boston Massacre in 1770, working to prevent violence.

His leadership skills were apparent as he rose from a militia troop, a soldier in the Continental Army, a Colonel of artillery, and eventually rose to the Army's General, replacing George Washington.

He led a mission to Fort Ticonderoga to retrieve captured British artillery. The winter mission resulted in sixty tons of artillery transported over 300 miles in hazardous conditions to Boston, where they were used to drive the British out of the city.

Henry Knox's success prepared him and his men for the action that reinvigorated Colonial spirits with the attitude that victory was possible.

Christmas night, 1776, General Washington led his troops across the Delaware River, including Colonel Knox and his artillerymen. The Trenton victory would not have been possible without Knox and his troops providing Washington the firepower to launch the audacious day-after-Christmas attack. He was promoted to Brigadier General for his leadership there.

Knox was an essential and dependable leader for the remainder of the Revolutionary War. After the war, he served five years as the second Secretary of War. His leadership was instrumental in dealing with Native Americans as the country expanded. Knox did not return to the bookstore after completing his military and public service at the end of 1794.

Benefitting from the reputation he built serving the country, he invested in real estate, cattle, lumber, and shipbuilding, among others, with mixed results. Knox accomplished much because he refused to accept others' definitions of who he was and what he could do. His example is worthy of our emulation.

The vital lesson for us is this: where we begin our journey doesn't determine where we end life. Our dreams, efforts, determination, persistence, overcoming adversity, serving humanity, and collaborating with others enable us to grow and increase achievements throughout our days. We can determine what we accomplish with faith in God and ourselves.

HENRY KNOX QUOTES

"We want great men who, when fortune frowns, will not be discouraged."

"Every friend to the liberty of his country is bound to reflect, and step forward to prevent the dreadful consequences which shall result from a government of events."

"We shall cut no small figure throughout the country with our cannon."

MERCY OTIS WARREN

"The rights of the individual should be the primary object of all governments."

While the vast majority of founders and patriots that we are aware of are men, more women than we know contributed mightily to the quest for independence in a multitude of manners.

Mercy Otis Warren (September 28, 1728 – October 19, 1814) was an excellent example of such a woman. She was a thought leader who influenced people with poems, plays, and pamphlets, advocating the independence position in public discussion.

She was born to a mother descended from a Mayflower pilgrim and James Otis, a farmer, lawyer, and pre-war patriot father. Her parent's hostile views toward the British predated the independence movement. They ensured she received a complete education from tutors rather than formal institutions and encouraged her quest for learning and independent thought.

Her marriage to James Warren, who also contributed to patriot efforts, further supported her thinking, speaking, and writing activities. Her initial Boston newspaper articles in 1772 stoked the flames of anti-British sentiment, as did the play *The Adulateur*. Like so many writers during the period, she published her plays and writings anonymously, reaching additional audiences with patriot themes.

Mercy's further actions progressed to protests and participating in the formation of the committees on correspondence, which served as the glue to unite the colonies. She supported her husband's wartime actions while continuing to influence the Revolution with her writings and raising their family.

After the war, she and her husband were anti-federalists during the debates on The Constitution, believing in state supremacy over the federal government. They advocated and worked to add the Bill of Rights to the Constitution.

Mercy lifted the anonymity of her writing in 1790, but she wasn't through adding her opinion to the public discourse. In 1805, she published *History of the Rise, Progress and Termination of the American Revolution*. It emphasized the anti-federalist beliefs of Thomas Jefferson and drew criticism from John Adams and the Federalists.

Warren was a reluctant commentator on the issues of the day until friends encouraged her to add her voice and its unique viewpoint. Her works added historical background and moral lessons, inspiring more citizens to join the independence movement. She is another example that each of us can positively add to the growth and success of our family, country, and posterity.

She is worthy of our remembrance and appreciation as her uncommon perspective and style contributed to our individual rights and the freedoms we enjoy today.

MERCY OTIS WARREN QUOTES

"The origin of all power is in the people, and they have an incontestable right to check the creatures of their own creation."

"No republic ever yet stood on a stable foundation without satisfying the common people."

"Democratic principles are the result of equality of condition."

"The bulk of mankind have indeed, in all countries in their turn been made the prey of ambition."

"The study of the human character opens at once a beautiful and a deformed picture of the soul."

"The waves have rolled upon me, the billows are repeatedly broken over me, yet I am not sunk down."

FRANCIS MARION
"THE SWAMP FOX"

"I am in love and my sweetheart is Liberty. Be that heavenly nymph my companion, and these woods shall have charms beyond London and Paris in slavery.

To have no proud monarch driving over me with his gilt coaches; nor his host of excise-men and tax-gatherers insulting and robbing me; but to be my own master, my own prince and sovereign, gloriously preserving my national dignity, and pursuing my true happiness.

Planting my vineyards, and eating their luscious fruits; and sowing my fields, and reaping the golden grain: and seeing millions of brothers all around me, equally free and happy as myself.

This, sir, is what I long for."

While most perceive the majority of the action during the Revolutionary War occurred in the North, Francis Marion (?, 1732 – February 27, 1795), also known by his actions as The Swamp Fox, after evading the British for twenty-six miles through the swamps of South Carolina, and his militia force proved that narrative incomplete.

He led troops in the South unconventionally in more battles, sacrificing more patriots and contributing a disproportionate benefit to the independence movement.

Though he was born into a family that operated a plantation, his primary education resulted from hands-on experience rather than theories in books. He went to sea at fifteen and survived a shipwreck and a week in the ocean before rescue. He later managed the family property before enlisting in the militia during the French and Indian War.

Soon after Lexington and Concord, Marion was commissioned into the Continental Army. After the 1776 action at Fort Sullivan, he was elevated to the rank of Lieutenant Colonel.

Action in the Southern theater escalated in 1780 with a change in British strategy. Marion avoided capture in the siege of Charleston and created a small force that harassed the British using what is called today guerilla tactics, which he is credited as its father in America. His men were true volunteers providing all their supplies in addition to fighting.

He led troops and fought in twelve battles and actions in the succeeding two years. Marion's militia relied on surprise, civilian clothing, and fighting for their freedom to inspire men to sacrifice more, fight harder, and persevere during trying times to achieve victory. The support his force provided to the Continental Army's regulars contributed to the defeat of the British in the South, which received formal recognition from the Continental Congress.

After the war, Marion was elected to the South Carolina General Assembly, where he served briefly before returning to his plantation. Later, he was elected and served in the state senate.

His legacy includes ships, universities, schools, national forests, and parks named after him. Books, television shows, and movie portrayals showcase his courage and leadership. Marion largely inspired Mel Gibson's character in *The Patriot*. Seventeen counties and twenty-nine towns bear his name. He and the freedom fighters he led were celebrated throughout the colonies for their efforts, and Marion's reputation was only surpassed by George Washington.

Francis Marion quotes

"More battles, engagements, and skirmishes were fought in South Carolina during the Revolution than in any other colony. Conservative estimates place the number of combat actions in the state at more than two hundred, a third of all that took place in the entire war.

No other colony had as many inches of its territory affected by battle; of the state's forty-six present-day counties, forty-five ended up seeing Revolutionary War actions.

Nearly 20 percent of all Americans who died in battle in the Revolution died in South Carolina in the last two years of the war."

***

"To expect defeat is nine-tenths of defeat itself. It becomes a self-fulfilling prophecy.

It is best to plan for all eventualities then believe in success, and only cross the failure bridge if you come to it!"

***

"Who can doubt that God created us to be happy, and thereto made us to love one another? It is plainly written as Gospel.

The heart is sometimes so embittered that nothing but Divine love can sweeten it, so enraged that devotion can only becalm it, and so broken down that it takes all the forces of heavenly hope to raise it.

In short, the religion of Jesus Christ is the only sure and controlling power over sin."

***

"Every man carries with him the world in which he must live."

"No one person can possibly combine all the elements supposed to make up what everyone means by friendship."

"Promises that you make to yourself are often like the Japanese plum tree – they bear no fruit."

"What a strange pattern the shuttle of life can weave."

LEADERS

Liberty Bell and Independence Hall

"We want great men (and women) who, when fortune frowns, will not be discouraged."

—Henry Knox

"Liberty when it begins to take root, is a plant of rapid growth."
—George Washington

James Forten

"Our country asserts for itself the glory of being the freest upon the surface of the globe... but one dark spot still dimmed its lustre. Domestic slavery existed among a people who had themselves disdained to submit to a master."

Born free, when so many of his race were enslaved people in the United States, did not deliver an easy life to James Forten (September 2, 1766 – March 4, 1842). His success required the exact ingredients needed by others and in larger doses to overcome the additional obstacle of race.

James' father died when he was seven leading him to work a variety of entry-level jobs to help his family. Formal schooling was forfeited to survive the game of life.

At fourteen, in the depth of the Revolutionary War, Forten signed on to the *Royal Louis* captained by Stephen Decatur Sr. His primary job during combat was as a powder boy, resupplying the cannon crews on multiple levels with gunpowder. Failure to move about the ship quickly enough would expose men to death and the vessel to sinking or surrender.

The British Navy captured his ship, and James joined the crew on a British prison ship for seven months before he was granted freedom in a prisoner exchange on the promise of not returning to the war. He sailed to England and worked in the shipping industry, returning to Philadelphia in 1790.

James's experience and quality work ethic on ships opened the door to apprenticing as a sailmaker. When his employer retired in 1798, James bought the enterprise, and by 1810, he was one of the wealthy men in Philadelphia. His employment of people of all races foretold his future efforts for humankind.

Being established and prosperous enabled Forten to stand up in a leadership role advocating the end of slavery in the early 19th century, including forming the American AntiSlavery Society in his house in 1833. He signed petitions, wrote pamphlets, spoke out for the growing abolitionist movement, financially supported churches, and participated in other efforts to benefit people of color, and served as an example to succeeding generations that all people could achieve the American dream.

James Forten's legacy is worth everyone knowing and striving to impact others equally. He was forced to work by seven, participated in the Revolutionary War, apprenticed a trade, bought and built a business empire, served his community and fellow citizens in many ways over several years, and left generations of family members inspired to carry on his service to others.

GILBERT STUART

The Athenaeum

*"What a business is this of a portrait painter! You bring him
a potato and expect he will paint you a peach."*

Long before any cameras, and especially hand-held
communication devices that include cameras, portrait painters
created images of people, landscapes, and events that enable us to
visualize their subjects today. John Trumbull and Charles Wilson
Peale were among the most notable portait painters during the
founding of the United States.

People recognized Gilbert Stuart's (December 3, 1755 – July
9, 1828) gift for painting when he was six years old. His work to

develop his talent led him to move to Great Britain when he was sixteen where he continued to develop his skills until returning to America in 1793.

He set an early goal to paint George Washington, recognizing the opportunity to provide financially for his family from ongoing print sales. Stuart strategically painted individuals who might catch Washington's attention, which finally occurred in 1796.

While he painted nearly 1,000 portraits, including multiple images of Washington, the unfinished Washington painting, known as *The Athenaeum*, is the most recognized and popular.

The Athenaeum has its own unique history, which gained Stuart further acclaim. In 1869, the image started appearing on one-dollar bills and continues today. In 1932, the picture was distributed to virtually every school classroom to celebrate Washington's 200th birthday.

A second portrait of Washington was named the **Lansdowne** portrait because it was given to former British Prime Minister William Petty, the first Marquees of Landsdowne. It shows Washington standing beside a writing table with his right hand extended. While well known, the painting did not return to the United States until 2001, when the National Portrait Gallery purchased it for 20 million dollars.

Another version of the *Landsdowne* hung in the White House, where First Lady, Dolly Madison, saved it from fire when the British burned the White House in 1814.

Stuart died in poverty, as have so many creative artists. An effort to raise money for his family included the first public showing of *The Athenaeum*, which became his most celebrated work.

Gilbert Stuart's reputation made him the painter everyone wanted to commission for their paintings. Art experts credit Stuart with developing the American style of portraits, which we still admire and appreciate.

Jonathan Edwards

"He who does not know Him, knows nothing else as it truly is."

Though he did not live to see the Revolutionary War and the establishment of an independent United States, Jonathan Edwards (October 5, 1703 – March 22, 1758) positively influenced the Founders and their parent's generation.

Jonathan was the only boy in his family that included ten sisters. His maternal grandfather was an influential pastor setting an example and shaping Jonathan's early life and education. He received a classical education at home, including Greek, Latin, and Hebrew. At an early age, he demonstrated a special interest and aptitude for spiritual matters.

At thirteen, Edwards entered Yale College, earning an undergraduate degree in four years and, two years later, one in theology.

He dedicated his life to serving God convicted people should experience truth in their hearts in addition to their minds. He delivered messages quietly in a tone relying on the power of the text to attract listeners and converts.

Before the American Revolution, it was common for colonies to sanction Christian church denominations, which inhibited them from coming together in any cooperative effort.

The Holy Spirit provided Edwards with biblical knowledge, critical thinking ability, a servant's heart, and love and desire to serve God. His writings and sermons moved people contributing to a celebrated revival known as the Great Awakening (1730 – 1755), which brought previously separated church denominations together. Many recognize Edwards as its first unofficial leader.

Unknown at the time but evident later, Edwards's messages on repentance, salvation, and justification by faith bridged the differences of several denominations creating common ground for the thirteen colonies to work together for their mutual independence and liberty from England.

After leaving his church in 1750, he spent his remaining years as a missionary to the Native Americans, where his wife and eleven children participated in the mission work. He wrote some of his most influential works after leaving his ministry and was named president of Princeton College shortly before his death from smallpox.

We see Edwards in history for his achievements and influence on all generations, even to this day. He encouraged people to seek salvation based on Biblical text, highlighted the importance of missions, and preached living justified by faith.

It is easy to overlook his courage and conviction, faithfully speaking against the accepted doctrine of the day, which caused him to lose his church and those desiring a less demanding religion.

Providence touched Jonathan Edwards, who stirred the souls of countless millions. Without his contribution to bringing state-sanctioned church denominations closer together, which influenced the American Independence movement, it is possible we might still be British subjects. We continue to benefit from his life, as will generations who follow us.

JONATHAN EDWARDS QUOTES

"Truth is the agreement of our ideas with the ideas of God."

"It is the duty of God's people to trust in him when in darkness."

"When indeed it is in God we live, and move, and have our being. We cannot draw a breath without his help."

"Prayer is as natural an expression of fatih as breathing is of life."

"When God is about to do a mighty new thing, He always sets His people to praying."

"God's purpose for my life was that I have a passion for God's glory and that I have a passion for my joy in that glory, and that these two are one passion."

"We must view humility as one of the most essential things that characterizes true Christianity."

"Nothing sets a person so much out of the devil's reach as humility."

"He who has Christ has all he needs and needs no more."

Eli Whitney

"I never thought my cotton gin would change history."

Most people familiar with Eli Whitney (Dec. 8, 1765 – Jan. 8, 1825) are only aware of his world-changing invention of the cotton gin (1793).

Like so many other great leaders, his influence on the world of his day, and the future, was far more significant than ever imagined at the time or remembered today.

It is common for people to view others within narrow ranges of their whole person and for us to do likewise. Limiting our understanding of people's capabilities and interests restricts our ability to collaborate, benefitting both parties and often untold others with our efforts.

Eli Whitney is a wonderful example of someone who changed the world in multiple ways, but is generally recognized for only one accomplishment.

Eli grew up on a farm, but his interest and gift for mechanical things revealed itself during his boyhood. He not only made nails during the Revolutionary War but did so on a device he invented for more efficiency.

Like many of the period, he pursued the law, first graduating from Yale and then reading the law while working on the plantation of the late General Nathaniel Greene in Georgia.

Providence placed Whitney in the right spot at the right time to encourage the application of his mechanical skills. Eli observed the South's economic challenges from the tobacco crop's decline. Planters recognized cotton as a potential replacement, but labor costs and the time to process it reduced its appeal.

Whitney secured approval to defer his studies to focus on a device to process cotton faster, applying for a patent in October 1793. The cotton gin was an immediate success in transforming Southern agriculture, making cotton king, and benefiting the slave industry instead of hurting it as Whitney desired.

Like many other inventors, his inexperience in business and patent law enabled others to gain much of the wealth from its creation and improvement, leaving Whitney with the fame of his invention.

"Necessity is the mother of invention," Aesop tells us, and Whitney found it necessary to find a path to restoring and providing for his financial needs. He determined his best opportunity lay securing a government contract to supply muskets. Like the production challenge with cotton, everyone at that time produced muskets manually one-at-a-time increasing costs and delaying delivery.

Whitney foresaw the advantage of mass-producing interchangeable parts that would speed assembly, reduce costs, and improve national security. Despite his skills, results took years to occur.

He is credited with creating milling machines to more efficiently manufacture parts enabling mass production, which sped the American Industrial Revolution benefitting all citizens then, today, and for the future.

Eli Whitney demonstrated it doesn't matter your circumstances at birth, education, or early achievements, but persistent growth, tenacity, and effort can result in achievements that change the world.

Charles Wilson Peale

"The learner must be led always from familiar objects toward the unfamiliar guided along, as it were, a chain of flowers into the mysteries of life."

Charles Wilson Peale (April 15, 1741 – February 22, 1827) is most known for painting more than 1100 portraits, (including many of George Washington who sat for him 14 times) and establishing one of the first museums in the United States. However, he was much more of an AmeriCAN than those triumphs alone.

He could be described today as a Renaissance man achieving success as a famous portrait painter, soldier, inventor, scientist, author, politician, and family man.

He began humbly as an apprentice saddle maker after his father's death when he was thirteen. Like so many other successful people, he discovered saddle making, working with clocks, and silversmithing was not his calling. He finally found his true talent as a portrait painter.

Peale's progression in painting serves as an example to all of us of the need to water and fertilize talent with ingenuity, study, determination, financial and spiritual encouragement from others, persistence through adversity, and outside influences to achieve unparalleled success in any field.

Charles traded a saddle for introductory painting lessons and impressed Maryland art lovers enough to sponsor him studying art in England for three years. Upon his return he joined the growing independence movement providing him a wealth of movers and shakers to paint.

Charles served in the Pennsylvania Assembly during the war, which slowed his painting business, but his service in the state militia resulted in the opposite outcome. Charles rose to the rank of Captain, recruited troops, and participated in multiple battles before returning to his painting efforts.

First opening a painting gallery during the war, Peale eventually opened one of the first museums in America, which became the Philadelphia Museum. It exhibited his artwork and other collections, in addition to the first complete mastodon skeleton discovered on an expedition he participated in and eventually chronicled with a painting. Others, including P.T. Barnum, copied and expanded on his ideas, influencing many of the great museums in the country.

Like Gilbert Stuart and John Trumbull, Peale's portraits give us a glimpse at the Founders, patriots, and AmeriCANS who birthed America, enabling us to look into their faces and souls.

It is important we see those who paid the down payment for our liberty to instill the responsibility into us to repay them and those since then by preserving, advancing, and passing that gift to future generations.

Peale's appeal (yes, the pun is intended) is that he lived the American dream without knowing that he did it. He was not content to remain in his initial field of work nor restrict his success to his most notable profession either. Charles continuously worked to improve himself, living life to the fullest and leaving an excellent example and legacy.

Daniel Boone

"Having an exciting destination is like setting a needle in your compass. From then on, the compass only knows one point – it's ideal. And it will faithfully guide you there through the darkest nights and fiercest storms."

Few people in history achieved the name recognition and reputation Daniel Boone earned (November 2, 1734 – September 26, 1820), but like many AmeriCANS, his achievements were broader and more significant than we routinely remember.

Unlike most of the Founders, he was born into a modest Quaker family of eleven children. Though he learned to read and write, his primary education prepared him for his adventures as a trapper and explorer who blazed trails and made the frontier more tolerable for those who followed.

Boone was a natural leader serving three terms in the Virginia General Assembly, founding Boonesboro, Kentucky, and rising to the rank of Captain in the militia during the Revolutionary War. His charisma and dependability attracted people to follow him, and history affirmed their choice repeatedly.

The primary events Boone experienced during the war include the kidnapping and rescue of his daughter and another girl in 1776, Daniel's capture and escape from the Indians to warn Boonesboro of an impending attack in 1778, and the Battle of Blue Licks in 1782, where his son, Israel, was killed. His daughter's kidnapping was the basis of James Fenimore Cooper's *The Last of the Mohicans*. Boone's escape and 160-mile return to Boonesboro in five days to save the town and solidify the settling of Kentucky was an incredible feat of determination and overcoming physical challenges.

Multiple home relocations, various jobs, and continued public service marked Boone's post-war life. Daniel operated a tavern and a trading post, he traded horses, and speculated on land; he was a surveyor and Lieutenant Colonel in the militia and served again in the Virginia State Assembly. He participated in a six-month hunt when he was 76 years old that traversed more than 2,000 miles from the area around St. Louis to the Yellowstone area and back.

The Boone family lived in Kentucky, present-day West Virginia, and Spanish Louisiana, which is currently part of Missouri, to be closer to their children and grandchildren.

Daniel Boone died and was buried in Missouri, but his story didn't end there. In death, as in life, Daniel Boone's experience was unique. Multiple burials, questionable grave markings, and time bring us to today where cemeteries in both Kentucky and Missouri claim to be the final resting place of Daniel Boone.

He was larger than life in so many ways, and lived life to the fullest until the end. His lifetime of serving others is worthy of our emulation.

DANIEL BOONE QUOTES

"It isn't how you die. It's what you live for."

"The religion I have to love and fear God, believe in Jesus Christ, do all the good to my neighbor, and myself I can, do as little harm as I can help, and trust on God's mercy for the rest."

"Curiosity is natural to the soul of man and interesting objects have a powerful influence on our affections."

"I've opened the way for others to make fortunes, but a fortune for myself was not what I was after."

Chief Pontiac

"It is important that we unite now more than ever so that our common enemies do not take advantage of us."

Chief Pontiac (1714 or 1720 – April 20, 1769) illustrates for us that exceptional leadership is not restricted by race, culture, or time but instead demonstrates distinct traits regardless of any differences or the circumstances one finds themselves in when called to lead.

Few facts are certain about Pontiac's parents or childhood, which the discrepancy in his birth year confirms. He rose to war leadership by 1747, and his authority continued to grow through the French and Indian War, during which he supported the French.

After the French defeat, Pontiac recognized the threat of British migration into tribal lands and the necessity of coordinating Indian tribes to repel the invasion successfully.

Pontiac's success resulted from uniting several tribes to fight British encroachment on their tribal lands in what became known as "Pontiac's War" in 1763-1764. His victories would not have been possible without learning from his ancestor's experience, his reputation as an honorable leader, persuading several tribes of the advantage of unity and teamwork, and their perseverance to win their objectives before overwhelming British strength forced them to negotiate peace.

Mixed results marked his final years, and an assassin cowardly clubbed and stabbed him from behind in 1769. Like everyone, he experienced successes and failures, achievements and shortcomings. Rather than cancel him because of the imperfection of his humanity, we should celebrate and learn from his contributions to the human spirit and understand and avoid repeating his inadequate actions.

He longed to protect, serve, and improve tribal life and risked his personal safety and comfort by acting on that desire repeatedly. His actions lifted his people's spirit and lifestyle.

Pontiac's leadership is worthy of our study, remembrance, and honor. Thankfully, several cities are named Pontiac, and his name adorned a famous automobile brand for many years. No one knows the number of people changed forever by the ideals he lived and his leadership example.

Pontiac Quotes

"It is important for us, as Native Americans, to remember our ancestors and traditions. We must keep them alive so that our children can continue to learn from their wisdom."

"Animals run from dangers they know, while civilized men run away from dangers they ignore."

"A great human has died today; honor him for what he achieved."

"We must never stop until we have fulfilled our destiny."

Phyllis Wheatley

"In every human Beast, God has implanted a Principle, which we call Love of Freedom; it is impatient of Oppression, and pants for Deliverance."

Not all the voices crying for independence in the 1770s were from people calling for the same cultural and societal change. Nor did all leaders utilize the same techniques to influence people's actions, changing lives and impacting future generations of Americans.

Like other places and times, progress in the 18th century moved in a non-linear path led and guided by many souls. Phyllis Wheatley (1753 – December 5, 1784) is another example of one of the few whom people would have expected to achieve her heights and touch multitudes with her wisdom.

***

Phyllis was born in West Africa and bound there as a girl before being shipped to Boston, where a tailor named John Wheatley and his wife acquired her. Unlike so many enslaved people, the Wheatley's taught her to read and write, and within two years, she also mastered Greek and Latin.

As a teenager, she began expressing herself in poetry and quickly received recognition for her literary and thinking skills. Phyllis published her poems beginning in 1767, commenting on various topics, including slavery, gaining her Christian faith, George Whitfield, and the independence movement.

The Wheatley's sent her to London with their son, hoping to increase her opportunity to publish her works. *Poems on Various Subjects, Religious and Moral,* first appeared in 1773, generating immediate acclaim. She was the first African-American to publish a book.

Wheatley returned from London and was freed by the Wheatley family in 1774. She married John Peters and took his name in 1778. Their life as freed blacks demanded income generation, which reduced her writing efforts. Phyllis birthed three children, all of whom died in childhood, and she passed away at thirty-one, believed to be from childbirth complications.

Phyllis Wheatley's life and writings changed people's beliefs about the capabilities of African-Americans in her lifetime, and the papers she left behind continue to influence people today. Her example affirms regardless of the person or endeavor, we never know the impact beyond our lifetime our efforts to lift people's spirits and influence generations will have on the future.

PHYLLIS WHEATLEY QUOTES

"The world is a severe schoolmaster, for its frowns are less dangerous than its smiles and flatteries, and it is a difficult task to keep in the path of wisdom."

"Thou didst, in strains of eloquence refin'd, Inflame the soul, and captivate the mind."

"Though thickest gloom look back, immortal shade, On that confusion which thy death has made."

"Imagination! who can sing thy force? Or who describe the swiftness of thy course? Soaring through air to find the bright abode, Th' empyreal palace of the thund'ring God, We on thy pinions can surpass the wind, And leave the rolling universe behind."

"Enlarge the close contracted mind, And fill it with thy fire."

A Note from the Author

Battle of Lexington – 1775   Surrender at Yorktown - 1781
By William Barnes Wollen   By John Trumbull

True AmeriCANS hearts race when they read about the heroes on whose shoulders we stand today. Goosebumps rise on their skin when they hear *Yankee Doodle, The Star Spangled Banner,* and other patriotic songs.

AmeriCANS are **grateful** for the gift of being Americans, take their **responsibility** of citizenship seriously, are **confident** and **optimistic** about living the American dream with **Liberty**, and **are committed** to leaving our beloved country and descendants an even better life.

***

As an American, we are blessed to have a choice in the life we live.

Will we travel day-by-day only living for self and pleasure?

Or, will we honor our ancestors, serve our families, friends, and communities, and extend the gift of freedom we received without merit to future generations?

Every day presents another choice and decision for us.

It is never too late to begin, but it is always too early to quit repaying our gift.

***

In the Afterword of Mary Beth Norton's book, *1774, The Long Year of the Revolution*, she quoted a poem published in two newspapers titled *The Glorious 74*. I can find no reference to its author.

I appreciate the entire poem, which was set to the British song, *Hearts of Oak*, but I love the body of its ending, which says in part:

"With sons whom I've fostered and cherished of your,
Their freedom shall flourish till time is no more;

No tyrant shall rule them tis heaven's decree,
They shall never be slaves when they dare to be free."

May we live such lives and return the favor given us to future generations!

Bibliography

Addison, Joseph, *Cato: A Tragedy*, a play, 1712.

The Alamo movie, Batjac Productions, 1960.

https://www.archives.gov/.

https://www.battlefields.org.

http://www.biography.com.

https://www.britannica.com/.

Byrne, Kerry, https://www.foxnews.com/lifestyle/meet-american-who-led-77-minutemen-against-700-redcoats-battle-lexington-captain-john-parker, April 14, 2023.

https://www.catholicworldreport.com/.

Chernow, Ron, *Alexander Hamilton*, City of Westminster, London, Penquin Press, 2004.

https://clipart-library.com/.

https://www.colonialwilliamsburg.org.

https://commons.wikimedia.org/wiki/Main_Page.

Cunningham, Noble E. Jr., *The Life of Thomas Jefferson*, New York, Ballantine Books, 1987.

https://diplomaticrooms.state.gov/exhibits/the-first-american-diplomat-benjamin-franklin/.

Drury, Bob and Clavin, Tom, *Valley Forge*, New York, Simon & Schuster, 2018.

Ellis, Joseph J., *Founding Brothers: The Revolutionary Generation*, New York, Vintage Books, 2000.

Ellis, Joseph J., *His Excellency: George Washington*, New York, Vintage Books, 2004.

https://fee.org/articles/dr-joseph-warren-the-founding-father-who-fought-for-liberty-at-bunker-hill-and-paid-with-his-life/.

https://www.findagrave.com.

The First American, Gingrich Productions, 2016.

Fischer, David Hackett, *Washington's Crossing,* Oxford, Oxford Press, 2004.

Franklin, Benjamin, *Poor Richard's Almanack*, Philadelphia, various editions, 1733-1758.

https://www.grabmyessay.com/foundingfatherquotes-com.

https://www.happybetterwiser.com/quotes.

https://history.com.

https://honoringourpatriots.dar.org/patriots/anna-smith-strong/.

https://inspirationandexploration.com.

Kaminski, John P., *The Founders on the Founders*, Charlottesville, U.Va. Press ed., 2008. Robert Morris to Horatio Gates.

http://www.Kids.britannica.com.

Langguth, A. J., *Patriots: The Men Who Started the American Revolution*,

New York, Simon & Schuster, 1988.

Legends and Lies – The Patriots: Sam Adams and Paul Revere – The Rebellion Begins, Ajax Broome, executive producer, 2016.

https://www.loc.gov/free-to-use/.

Lossing, B.J., *The Lives of The Signers of the Declaration of Independence*, Aledo, Reprint by Wallbuilders Press, 1995.

McCullough, David, *John Adams*, New York, Simon & Schuster, 2001.

https://marbleheadhistory.org/spirit-of-76-painting/.

https://mtsu.edu/first-amendment/article/801/established-churches-in-early-america.

https://newenglandhistoricalsociety.com.

Norton, Mary Beth, *1774: The Long Year of the Revolution*, New York, Knopf, 2020.

http://www.onthisday.com.

https://originalfoundingfathers.com/.

Paine, Thomas, *Common Sense*, Philadelphia, 1776.

Paine, Thomas, *Rights of Man*, Philadelphia, 1791.

Paine, Thomas, *The Age of Reason*, Philadelphia, 1794.

Paine, Thomas, *The American Crisis*, Philadelphia, 1776.

https://parade.com/1328166/shameikarhymes/african-american-historical-figures/.

https://patriotpost.us/alexander/3467-the-patriots-primer-on-american-liberty-full-copyright-text-1996-09-17.

https://www.paulreverehouse.org/biography/.

https://www.quoteambition.com.

https://www.reveresriders.org/.

https://www.revolutionary-war.net/.

https://www.smithsonianmag.com/history.

Stoll, Ira, *Samuel Adams*, New York, Simon & Schuster, 2008.

https://www.supersummary.com/cato-a-tragedy/summary/.

https://www.thefamouspeople.com/18th-century-american-leaders.php.

https://theobjectivestandard.com/2018/03/act-worthy-of-yourselves-joseph-warren-on-defending-liberty/.

Thomas, Evan, *John Paul Jones*, New York, Simon & Schuster, 2003.

United States Constitution, 1787.

www.usni.org.

Wiersbe, Warren, *50 People Every Christian Should Know*, Grand Rapids, Baker Books, 2009.

https://www.womenshistory.org.

INDEX

Adams, President John 19, 56
Adams, Samuel 9, 19, 21, 52, 53, 54, 61, 65, 165
Adulateur, The 132
Aesop 148
Age of Reason, The 41, 165
The Alamo movie, 1960 24, 164
American AntiSlavery Society 140
Army 28, 29, 40, 61, 68, 89, 98, 99, 104, 105, 110, 111, 114, 116, 126, 129, 135
Andre, Major John 113, 115
Articles of Confederation 48, 71, 72, 89
American Crisis Number One, The 39, 40
The Athenaeum, painting 141, 142
Atlantic Ocean 65

Baltimore, Maryland 120, 121
Battle of Bunker Hill (Breed's Hill) 64
Battle of Monmouth 105
Bill of Rights, to The U.S. Constitution 48, 85, 86, 132
Bonhomme Richard 95, 96
Boone, Daniel 10, 153, 154, 155
Boonesboro, Kentucky 153, 154
Boston Harbor 102, 103
Boston Massacre 65, 108, 129
Boston Tea Party 61, 65, 68, 108
British Army 28, 61, 99, 111, 114, 126
British Navy 96, 140
Burr, Vice-President Aaron 68
Bush, President George W. 58

Canby, George 117
Castle William 103
Cato: A Tragedy 111, 164
Charleston, South Carolina 135
Chase, Samuel 9, 78, 79, 80, 81, 92
Chief Pontiac 2, 10, 17, 156
Christmas 16, 28, 40, 68, 129
Claypool, John 117
College of New Jersey 83
Common Sense 8, 40, 42, 120, 165, 172, 173
Concord, Massachusetts 37, 40, 61, 89, 102, 119, 126, 135
Constitutional Convention 50, 68, 71, 86

Continental Army 28, 29, 68, 104, 110, 114, 116, 129, 135
Continental Congress 44, 57, 58, 62, 71, 79, 83, 92, 93, 117, 121, 135
Continental Navy 96
Cooper, James Fenimore 154
Corbin, Margaret 105
Crockett, David 24
Culper Spy Ring 114

Dawes, William 65, 102
Decatur, Stephen St. 140
Declaration of Independence 2, 9, 18, 19, 20, 25, 31, 33, 39, 40, 53, 58, 60, 62, 64, 71, 72, 79, 83, 85, 89, 91, 93, 119, 120, 165
Delaware River 16, 28, 40, 129
Denmark 96
Disraeli, Benjamin 125

Eisenhower, President Dwight 124
Ellsworth, Oliver 72
England 33, 36, 39, 40, 53, 58, 89, 107, 108, 140, 144, 151

Federalist Papers 48, 68
Federalist Party 68, 75, 79, 80
First Continental Congress 57
Forten, James 10, 139, 140
Fort Sullivan 135
Fort Ticonderoga 129
France 33, 41, 58, 75, 92
Franklin, Benjamin 9, 19, 25, 31, 34
French and Indian War 28, 125, 135, 157
Friberg, Arnold 27

Gerry, Elbridge 65
Gettysburg Address 64
Gibson, Mel 136
The Glorious 74 163
Goddard Broadside 120
Goddard, Mary Katherine 10, 119, 120, 121
Grant, President U. S. 124
Great Awakening 144
Great Britain 14, 31, 53, 60, 96, 142
Greene, Nathaniel 2, 94, 148

Hale, Nathan 10, 21, 99, 110, 111, 112, 113, 114, 115
Hancock, John 9, 60, 61, 62, 65, 92, 102, 120, 126
Harrington, James 57
Hawaii 117
Hays, William 104
Hearts of Oak 163
History of the Rise, Progress and Termination of the American Revolution 132
Holmes, Oliver Wendell Jr. 11
Hopkinson, Francis 117
Howe, General Sir William 111, 115

Intolerable Acts 61

Jackson, President Andrew 76, 124
Jay, John 48
Jefferson, President Thomas 9, 19, 25, 43, 44, 45, 48, 49, 50, 58, 79, 80, 93, 94, 121, 132, 164
Jones, John Paul 10, 95, 96, 97, 165

Kennedy, President John F. 72
Kentucky 153, 154
King's College 68
Kitson, Henry Hudson 124, 127
Knox, General Henry 10, 128, 129, 130, 138

Last of the Mohicans, The 154
Lee, Billy 10, 17, 122, 123
Lee, Richard Henry 24
Lexington, Massachusetts 125
Lexington Minuteman statue, The 124, 127
Liberty Boys 107
Liberty Tree 108
Longfellow, Henry Wadsworth 102, 103
Louisiana Purchase 44

Madison, Dolly 49, 142
Madison, President James 21, 47
Marbury vs. Madison 75, 77
Marion, Francis, The Swamp Fox 10, 134, 135, 136
Marshall, John 9, 74, 75, 76
Martin, Joseph Plumb 105
Maryland Journal 119, 120

Maryland Supreme Court 79
Massachusetts 53, 57, 61, 62, 65, 125
Massachusetts Provincial Congress 65
McCullough vs. Maryland 76
Minutemen 61, 65
Missouri 154
Morris, Robert 10, 72, 88, 89, 90, 164
Mt. Vernon 123

National Archives 105
National Portrait Gallery 142
New Jersey 68, 83
New York 68, 99, 111, 114, 164, 165
New York Post 68
Norton, Mary Beth 163, 165

Pacific Ocean 44
Paine, Thomas 9, 19, 26, 39, 40, 41, 120, 165
Parliament 61
The Patriot, movie 136
Paul Revere's Ride 103
Peale, Charles Wilson 10, 141, 150, 151, 152
Pennsylvania 32, 33, 40, 89, 90, 151
Pennsylvania Magazine, The 40
Peters, John 160
Petty, William, British Prime Minister, and the first Marquees of Landsdowne 142
Pitcher, Molly 10, 104, 105
Poems on Various Subjects, Religious and Moral 160
Pontiac's War 157
Poor Richard's Almanack 33, 164
Porter, Horace 96
Prayer at Valley Forge, The 27
Princeton College 83, 144

Quaker 153

Revere, Paul 10, 61, 65, 101, 102, 103, 125, 165
Richardson, Ebenezer 108
Rights of Man, The 41
Roosevelt, President Theodore 93, 123, 124
Ross, Betsy 10, 17, 116, 117, 118
Ross, John 116
Russia 96

Saint Kitts and Nevis 67
Scotland 82, 83, 95
Seider (Snider), Christopher 10, 107, 108
Seneca 121
Serapis 95, 96
Setauket, Long Island 99
Sherman, Roger 9, 70, 71, 72, 73, 89
Sons of Liberty 61, 65, 107, 108
South Carolina 135, 136
South Carolina General Assembly 136
Spanish Louisiana 154
Spirit of '76, The 94
Stamp Act, 1765 37, 61, 86, 92
Star Spangled Banner, The 162
Statute of Virginia for Religious Freedom 44
Strong, Anna Smith 10, 98
Stuart, Gilbert 10, 49, 141, 142, 151

Tallmadge, Lt. Col. Benjamin 10, 113, 114, 115
Times of London, The 41
Thoughts on Government 57
Townshend Act 61
Trumbull, John 141, 151, 162

U.S. Constitution 33, 75
University of Virginia 44, 50

Valley Forge 27, 123, 164
Virginia 36, 37, 44, 48, 50, 75, 86, 153, 154
Virginia Constitution 37, 86
Virginia House of Burgesses 36, 86

War of 1812 44, 49
Warren, James 132
Warren, Dr. Joseph 9, 64, 65
Warren, Mercy Otis 10, 131, 133
Washington, President George 27
West Point 105, 115
West Virginia 154
Wheatley, John 160
Wheatley, Phillis 108
White House 49, 142
Whitfield, George 160
Whitney, Eli 10, 147, 148, 149
Willard, Archibald 94
Witherspoon, Dr. John 82

Wollen, William Barnes 162
Worcester vs. Georgia 76

Yale University Art Gallery 18
Yankee Doodle 162
Yellowstone 154

RICHARD V. BATTLE

Multi Award-Winning Author, Speaker,
Media Commentator and Advisor

Richard is the author of eleven books focused on communicating messages promoting God and Country and personal growth enabling people to pursue their dreams and fulfill their life's journey.

He has been a public speaker and trainer for over 30 years on leadership, motivation, faith, sales, and volunteerism.

Richard is an experienced corporate executive and non-profit leader who serves organizations in an advisory role.

Texas Governor Rick Perry appointed him to The Texas Judicial Council and The Texas Emerging Technology Fund.

As president of the Austin Junior Chamber of Commerce, the U.S. Junior Chamber of Commerce recognized the chapter as the Most Outstanding chapter in the United States. The Junior Chamber of Commerce International recognized Richard as the Outstanding Chapter President in the world.

He served on the board of directors of Alpha Kappa Psi, an international professional business fraternity, and was a past chairman.

He has served on the board of many organizations, including Shepperd Leadership Institute (past chairman), Boy Scouts of America, Muscular Dystrophy Association, and Keep Austin Beautiful.

Richard lives in Lakeway, Texas. His mission is to communicate Positive messages helping people win every day!

Aim High!
Work Hard!
NEVER Quit! ®

RICHARD V. BATTLE BOOKS

The Unopened Present

What life lessons do you want to teach your children? What if you do not live to communicate them?

Richard's son passed prematurely, leaving the 43 essential life lessons unopened.

Richard added commentary and depth to the 43 lessons from the letter, and the present awaits you to open.

It includes 50 Scriptures, 51 quotes, and 18 Battle's Bullets.

Available in paperback, Kindle, Nook, and audio editions.

Made in America
By AmeriCANS not AmeriCANTS

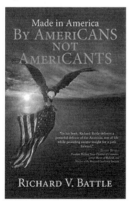

Made In America by AmeriCANS not AmeriCANTS is an uplifting volume providing readers the tools to learn, lead, and leave a legacy benefitting those who follow us.

If you want to fulfill your dreams and destiny, this book's AmeriCAN principles and examples will accelerate your quest.

It includes 103 quotes, 108 Battle's Bullets, and 135 Sage Sayings.

Available in paperback, Kindle, Nook, and audio editions.

Life's Daily Treasure
366 Doses of Hope, Optimism, Personal growth, and Encouragement

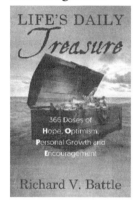

Does It Seem Like Hope Has Vanished? You're Not Alone – Here are 366 Daily Doses.

Life's Daily Treasure is for adults seeking hope and encouragement in an ever-challenging world.

It is a book of hope for today and every day and an excellent gift for all occasions!

Its 2,196 entries of inspiration, motivation, and American celebration are wonderful resources for speakers, pastors, teachers, and others.

Available in Hardback, Paperback, and Kindle editions.

Navigating Life's Journey
Common Sense in Uncommon Times

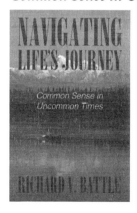

If you liked Conquering Life's Course, you'll love this successor to it.

Forty bite-sized, easy-to-read chapters of time-proven principles will restore your confidence in your beliefs, encourage you to defend them, and inspire you to teach your sacred values to your loved ones. It will lift your spirits and restore your hope in America.

It includes 250 examples and 75 motivational quotes.

Available in paperback, Kindle, and audio editions.

Conquering Life's Course
Common Sense in Chaotic Times

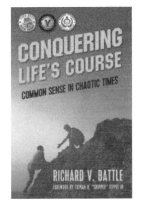

Do you wonder if Common Sense is vanishing?

It will entertain and inspire the reader to think, laugh and undertake actions to realize a more fulfilling life.

If you or a loved one have given up on understanding the world of today, Conquering Life's Course is a must-read. It assures readers that age-old traditions and wisdom still rule over unproven theories.

It is concise, easy to read, and offers invaluable insights that readers can share with the entire family.

Available in paperback, Kindle, and audio editions.

Unwelcome Opportunity –
Overcoming Life's Greatest Challenges

What do you do when you experience divorce, two heart procedures, and a cancer diagnosis within ten months? It is the story of an ordinary man facing multiple life challenges in one ten-month period.

In it, you will see an example of God's presence and provision that helped Richard Battle traverse this turbulent period of his life.

Available in paperback, Kindle, Nook, and audio editions.

Surviving Grief by God's Grace

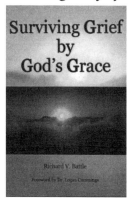

There is no greater loss in this world than losing one's child. This book is the first-person account of the author's loss of his first and then only child. It is a story of the grief, spiritual quest, and grace that helped Richard and his family survive and to live with hope for the future.

Available in paperback and Kindle editions.

The Four-Letter Word That Builds Character

Why are so many young people having a problem adapting to society today? Where have we gone wrong? Is it the parents or society in general? The Four-Letter Word That Builds Character can make a difference in this scattered and cluttered world. Based on the lessons learned from the author's first job and parental teaching of traditional values that have proven to be the foundation for lifelong success, this volume teaches 14 proven principles of a good work ethic and character.

Available in paperback, Kindle, and audio editions.

The Volunteer Handbook
How to Organize and Manage a Successful Organization

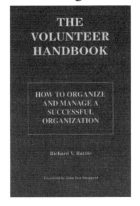

More than 75 topics provide specific ideas to help volunteer leaders maximize their efforts. Topics include Long-range, annual and event planning; Training board and prospective board members; how to recruit new members; ten steps to activate or reactivate a member; six steps to building a successful team; and How to motivate your membership. Effective Delegation. Managing non-performers.

Available in paperback

The Master's Sales Secrets
44 Strategies for Sensational Sales Success

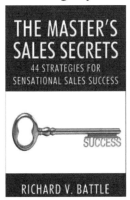

Richard V. Battle offers business leaders a graduate-level class in what he learned over forty-plus years in sales and sales management. It is Practical, sharp, and clearly communicated. The Master's Sales Secrets can be read cover to cover or referenced strategy by strategy.

Available in paperback and Kindle editions.

www.richardbattle.com

While I don't know where my path will lead me, I know the destination.

If you have suggestions for future ideas, or would like additional clarification on my efforts, you can reach me at richard@richardbattle.com.

Thank you again for your encouragement and support of my work.